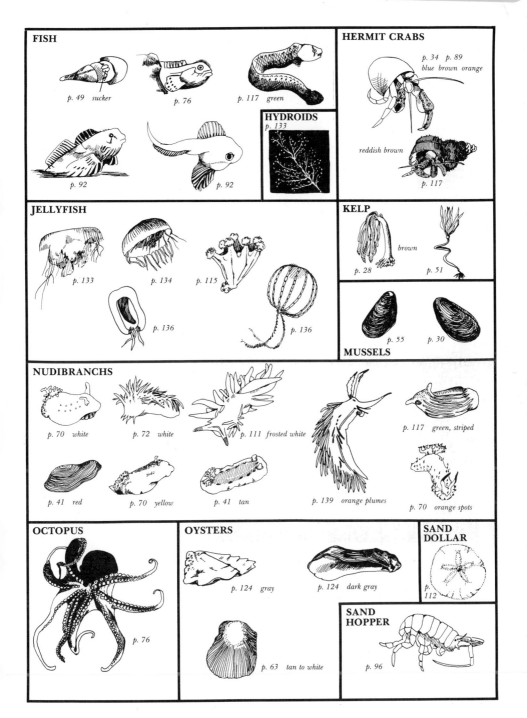

FISH

p. 49   sucker

p. 76

p. 117   green

p. 92

p. 92

HYDROIDS
p. 133

HERMIT CRABS

p. 34   p. 89
blue brown orange

reddish brown

p. 117

JELLYFISH

p. 133

p. 134

p. 115

p. 136

p. 136

KELP

brown

p. 28

p. 51

p. 55   p. 30

MUSSELS

NUDIBRANCHS

p. 70   white

p. 72   white

p. 111   frosted white

p. 117   green, striped

p. 41   red

p. 70   yellow

p. 41   tan

p. 139   orange plumes

p. 70   orange spots

OCTOPUS

p. 76

OYSTERS

p. 124   gray

p. 124   dark gray

p. 63   tan to white

SAND DOLLAR

p. 112

SAND HOPPER

p. 96

Living Shores

of the Pacific Northwest

By
Lynwood S. Smith

Photography by Bernard J. Nist and Lynwood S. Smith

PACIFIC
Search
BOOKS

715 Harrison Street, Seattle, WA 98109

Cover and Page Design by Lou Rivera
Drawings by Karel Hayes
All photographs are by Bernard Nist except those identified as the author's.

Cover Photo by Bernard Nist:
Cluster of giant barnacles *(Balanus nubilus)* found on exposed
rocky coast in mussel beds and under rocks and ledges in lower
intertidal zone, subtidally in San Juan Islands and Puget Sound.

Copyright © 1976 by Pacific Search
International Standard Book Number 0-914718-14-2
Library of Congress Catalog Card Number 76-17153
Manufactured in the United States of America

Contents

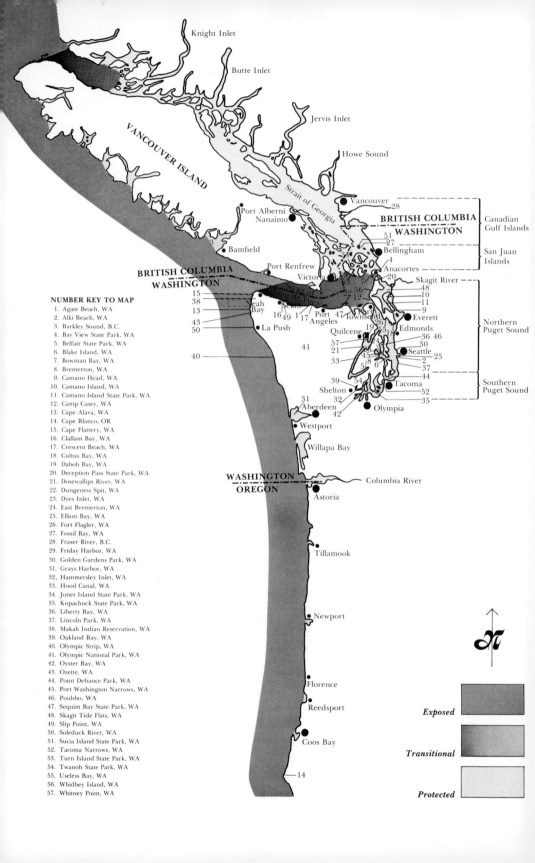

Knight Inlet

Butte Inlet

Jervis Inlet

Howe Sound

VANCOUVER ISLAND

Strait of Georgia

Vancouver — 28

Port Alberni
Nanaimo

BRITISH COLUMBIA
WASHINGTON

Canadian
Gulf Islands

51
27

Bamfield

Bellingham

San Juan
Islands

4
Anacortes
20

Port Renfrew

Victoria

Skagit River

NUMBER KEY TO MAP

1. Agate Beach, WA
2. Alki Beach, WA
3. Barkley Sound, B.C.
4. Bay View State Park, WA
5. Belfair State Park, WA
6. Blake Island, WA
7. Bowman Bay, WA
8. Bremerton, WA
9. Camano Head, WA
10. Camano Island, WA
11. Camano Island State Park, WA
12. Camp Casey, WA
13. Cape Alava, WA
14. Cape Blanco, OR
15. Cape Flattery, WA
16. Clallam Bay, WA
17. Crescent Beach, WA
18. Cultus Bay, WA
19. Dabob Bay, WA
20. Deception Pass State Park, WA
21. Dosewallips River, WA
22. Dungeness Spit, WA
23. Dyes Inlet, WA
24. East Bremerton, WA
25. Elliott Bay, WA
26. Fort Flagler, WA
27. Fossil Bay, WA
28. Fraser River, B.C.
29. Friday Harbor, WA
30. Golden Gardens Park, WA
31. Grays Harbor, WA
32. Hammersley Inlet, WA
33. Hood Canal, WA
34. Jones Island State Park, WA
35. Kopachuck State Park, WA
36. Liberty Bay, WA
37. Lincoln Park, WA
38. Makah Indian Reservation, WA
39. Oakland Bay, WA
40. Olympic Strip, WA
41. Olympic National Park, WA
42. Oyster Bay, WA
43. Ozette, WA
44. Point Defiance Park, WA
45. Port Washington Narrows, WA
46. Poulsbo, WA
47. Sequim Bay State Park, WA
48. Skagit Tide Flats, WA
49. Slip Point, WA
50. Soleduck River, WA
51. Sucia Island State Park, WA
52. Tacoma Narrows, WA
53. Turn Island State Park, WA
54. Twanoh State Park, WA
55. Useless Bay, WA
56. Whidbey Island, WA
57. Whitney Point, WA

BRITISH COLUMBIA
WASHINGTON

15
38
13
43
50

Neah
Bay

16 49 1 17

Port
Angeles

47

Port
Townsend

Everett

Northern
Puget Sound

La Push

Quilcene

Edmonds

36 46
30
Seattle
2
25

56
10
11
9

41

57
21
33

Southern
Puget Sound

40

39
Shelton
32

54

Tacoma

44

52
35

31
Aberdeen
42

Olympia

Westport

Willapa Bay

WASHINGTON
OREGON

Columbia River

Astoria

Tillamook

Newport

Florence

Reedsport

Coos Bay

14

Exposed

Transitional

Protected

How to use this book

This book is for people who are fascinated by seashore plants and animals but not by scientific names or complicated keys and classification. It is an attempt to present clearly the complexities and beauties of the seashore environments with a minimum of technical terminology. Using one of the four starting points below, you can easily find the names, importance, and lifestyles of the most common plants and animals of the beaches of Oregon, Washington, and British Columbia.

1. Picture Key (inside covers)

If you already have a plant or animal that you want to learn about, turn first to the inside covers. There you will find groups of pictures under such common names as crabs, clams, and starfish. Choose the illustration that looks most like your specimen. The number beside the picture is the page on which you will find your information.

2. Type of Beach

Beaches can be roughly classified as rocky, sandy, gravel, or mud. Section III describes the processes involved in the formation of these beaches, then discusses the common plants and animals on each. Beginning in Section IV, the top of each page indicates the kind of beach on which the specimen described is commonly found. While there are many variations of these basic types of beaches, you can usually decide which applies best to your situation. Then thumb through the book, looking for appropriate headings, common names, and pictures until you find your specimen. The common names at the top of the pages are the same as those used in the picture key.

3. Geographical Location

A. *Your Location.* Because no two beaches are alike, the beach you are visiting may have unique features. For this reason, this handbook features photos of representative public beaches and includes lists of similar beaches. If you have never visited one of these beaches, look at the map for locations.

B. *Geographical Distribution of Individual Species.* Different beaches accommodate different plants and animals; there are few species of seashore life that can live on all types of beaches. A list of all species described in this book in Table 1 indicates their distribution and abundance. Within their distribution, remember that you must also look for the particular animal or plant *on the proper kind of beach* — rocky, sandy, etc.

4. Vertical Distribution of Species

Most animals and plants live on a limited part of the beach. Only a few live near the high tide line; more live near the middle of the area between low and high tide levels (the intertidal zone); and most live near the low tide line. For example, periwinkle snails live near the high tide line and will drown if held underwater too long. Conversely, many animals living near the low tide line dry out and die if out of water for an hour or more. The species list in Table 2 shows the approximate vertical range for each of these plants and animals. This distribution — high, middle, or low — is similar regardless of whether the tidal range is six to eight feet (ocean beaches), ten to fifteen feet (Puget Sound), or twenty-five to thirty feet (as in some of the long inlets of British Columbia).

Appendix: Items for Later Reference

If you become fascinated with seashore life, you will want to know more about it than can possibly be squeezed into this small book. Therefore, a list of additional references on various aspects of seashore biology has been provided in Appendix 4 to suggest other outlets for your enthusiasm.

Beyond this, if your interest in seashore biology prompts you to seek a shell collection, to set up a marine aquarium, or to do anything that involves removing a creature from its natural habitat, you should also acquaint yourself with the laws concerning seashore animals. Appendix 3 lists names and addresses of several agencies with jurisdiction over the beaches. Many animals can be removed under various sport fishing regulations and limits; however, some are considered endangered species or are otherwise specially protected. Some areas are now or soon will be classed as sanctuaries, from which you are prohibited from removing anything. Among these conservation areas are state, provincial, and national parks. Know your local laws and follow them to help conserve the beaches for all to enjoy.

For some people, the major reason for a trip to the seashore is to find food. Appendix 1 lists standard ways to cook usual fare such as clams and crabs, then suggests a few other edible items for those with more adventurous tastes.

Finally, for those days when the weather is bad or the tides are wrong, there is a list of public aquariums (Appendix 2) where you can study marine animals in comfort, usually for only a modest admission price.

2

How to find seashore life

Seashores are places of such great variety that it is difficult to give simple, universal instructions for finding animals and observing their activities. The following suggestions may aid in your search:

Look on Rocks and Piling (Figures 1-3)

Most plants and animals are attached to something solid, either temporarily holding on or permanently cemented down. The majority live near the low tide line, because few can stand the long hours of exposure to summer sun and winter freezing. Thus, some rocks near the high tide line are nearly bare, except for a slippery coating of green slime and a few barnacles or periwinkle snails found in crevices. Pilings show a similar decrease in population density as you approach the high tide line, although most will be bare for their entire length until the creosote or other antifouling treatment has worn off.

9

1. Stable rocks at Slip Point, Wa.

Figure 1: This picture shows a series of large, fairly stable rocks at Slip Point on the Strait of Juan de Fuca. Near the high tide line exposure to the air is so severe and lengthy that only a few animals can survive on the shady, most protected, lower parts of the rock. Farther down the beach, both plants and animals are found living higher and higher on rocks' sides and tops because they spend less and less time exposed to the air during low tides. Finally, the lowest rocks are completely encrusted with organisms.

Figure 2: Rocky beaches are ideal for finding seashore plants and animals that need something solid for attachment. Since rocky beaches are scarce inside Puget Sound, don't overlook man-made breakwaters, but remember that such places are also very hazardous.

10

2. Breakwater at Edmonds, Wa.

3. Piling coated with mussels and barnacles

Figure 3: These piles have just begun to accumulate a coating of mussels and barnacles, which in another ten or twenty years will grow to accommodate a variety of animals several inches thick. The most populated piling may be found under old or abandoned docks. Because they are unsafe, be cautious.

11

Look under Rocks (Figures 4-6)

Any rock large enough to resist being moved by wave action during winter storms is a candidate for sheltering a wide variety of animals. In addition, water must be able to circulate freely when the rock is submerged. If it is embedded in sand or mud, there will be nothing under it except foul-smelling black mud containing hydrogen sulfide (which smells like rotten eggs) rather than oxygen. A pool of water under the rock may or may not enhance the numbers or variety of animals there. Look on the bottom side of the rock that you have turned over as well as where the rock formerly rested.

Figure 4: This shows the underside of a typical rock on a protected beach, revealing some creatures living under the rock and others attached to its underside. The colors of the organisms are typically muted or even drab.

Figure 5: A comparable rock on an exposed coastline houses brightly colored organisms: purple coralline algae resembling plaster; thinly spread, tan sponge; other coralline algae; several purple sea urchins; two chitons; and several patches of light brown colonial tunicates, which look and feel like hard gelatin.

Figure 6: The underside of a rock is sometimes overlooked when there is a well-populated pool of water underneath it. The bottom of this rock is covered with the eggs of a midshipman *(Porichthys notatus)* — the male fish guarding the eggs is in the pool (not shown) beneath the rock.

PLEASE NOTE: The environmental differences between top and bottom of the same rock are so great that turning over a rock and *leaving it upside down usually kills everything on both sides.* The animals formerly on top suffocate underneath, while the bottomside animals die of exposure on top. This is one of the major abuses whereby people destroy seashore environments.

Look in Holes, Cracks, and Crevices

Such places provide good protection from sun and drying and from flying rocks and debris during storms. Some animals, especially certain small clams, bore holes in rocks. After they die, many other clams occupy the holes. Similarly, a highly specialized clam, the shipworm or *Teredo,* bores holes in wood, which may later house other animals, such as small worms and sand hoppers.

12

Lynwood S. Smith

4. Underside of rock on protected beach

5. Underside of rock on exposed coastline

6. Bottom of rock covered with eggs of midshipman *(Porichthys notatus)*

13

Look in Tide Pools – Nature's Aquariums (Figure 7)

Pockets that remain filled with water while the tide is out usually collect and concentrate animals that are more widely dispersed when the tide is in. When these creatures see you, their first instinct is to scurry wildly about, find a hiding place, and remain perfectly still until it appears safe to move again. So you do the same — stay motionless and watch for crabs, shrimp, and fish as they begin to stir again. Also watch for sea anemones, sea cucumbers, tube worms, and others to relax and extend their tentacles. Wait to see whether snail shells contain snails or hermit crabs. This tide pool is spectacularly decorated with red sea urchins *(Strongylocentrotus franciscanus)*.

Dig in Sand, Gravel, Mud

Few plants and animals can survive on the surface of a sand, gravel, or mud beach if there are sufficiently large waves to keep the beach material moving constantly. On more protected beaches, however, there are lots of burrowing animals that live *in* the beach — clams, worms, and burrowing shrimp, for example.

The composition of a productive sandy/gravel beach typically consists of rocks, most of them less than four inches in diameter, and lots of loose pea gravel and sand. Water flows readily through the beach, clams can dig in it easily, and there are no black, smelly layers of decomposing mud. Dig slowly and wash each shovel of sand carefully. Straining the dug material through an eighth-inch or quarter-inch wire mesh screen often reveals many small items you would otherwise have missed.

The hole left by a clam digger does more damage by suffocating small clams under the gravel piled up around the hole than was done by digging the hole itself. On most clam beaches in Puget Sound and Hood Canal, the waves are *not* strong enough to level out the gravel again. It is a state law in Washington that all clam holes must be filled, a conservation measure difficult to enforce; clam diggers would improve their beaches by observing the law more consistently.

Look on, around, among, and under Larger Animals

On favorable beaches, there is always a shortage of living space, so little animals often live with larger ones. Look among barnacles or mussels (Figure 8) to find worms, sand hoppers, or small snails. Large starfish often carry small one- to two-inch scale worms (Figure 86), and large hermit crabs can harbor brightly striped worms as cohabitants of their snail shells. These animals are not parasites, just neighbors and hitchhikers.

14

7. Red sea urchins *(Strongylocentrotus franciscanus)* in tide pool

8. Barnacles, mussels, other sea creatures

Large Plants Support Whole Communities of Smaller Plants and Animals

Large brown seaweeds, commonly called kelp, have a rootlike structure, the holdfast, which is a labyrinth of holes, tunnels, and crevices that house many species of animals. A few encrusting-type animals live on the surface of the slippery, broad, leaflike part of the kelp (Figure 9). Eelgrass similarly hosts a variety of specialized tenants (Figure 10). Some colonial animals that look like plants — hydroids (Figure 141), for example — also house their quota of hitchhikers.

Look on and under Floats

Floating docks and other floating objects are a special kind of "beach" which is always close to the surface but never uncovered by low tide. Because the environment is so protected here, some of the seashore's most delicate and spectacular finery thrives (Figures 138-148).

9. Kelp, home for hitchhiking animals

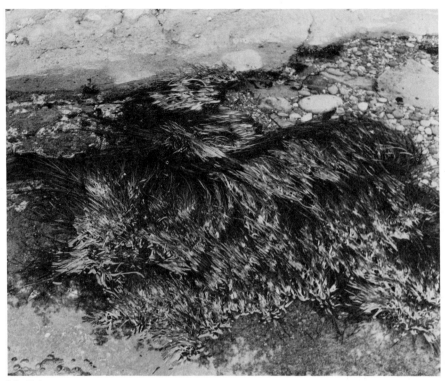

10. Eelgrass

Examine the Debris at the Tide Line at the Top of the Beach

Don't ignore the line of junk that high tide leaves behind. If you can't examine a beach at low tide, you can usually get a sample, admittedly somewhat battered, of what the waves have carried farther up. Piles of seaweed and eelgrass usually contain beach hoppers both in and underneath them — the odor doesn't seem to bother *them.*

Some of the floating material may have come from a considerable distance. For example, big rafts of floating kelp that originally grew along rocky shores south of the Oregon-California border come ashore on Washington beaches. Objects that have been afloat for a while also usually have types of animals living on them that are normally found only on the high seas — certain species of goose barnacles (similar to those in Figure 16), for example.

17

Touch What You See – Gently

Outside of obvious hazards like getting pinched by crabs, poked by sharp spines, cut on barnacles, nipped by a large worm, or stung by our one dangerous jellyfish (the sea blubber — large and reddish brown, with frilly, long tentacles, occurring here only in summer), it is almost impossible to get hurt by any of our local seashore animals. Touch provides information second only to sight in importance. You will find that a number of plants and animals look surprisingly similar, but feel quite different. For example, colonial sea squirts, encrusting sponge, coralline algae, and some encrusting brown seaweeds appear much alike, but coralline algae feel like rough plaster, while most other algae are firm but slippery. The colonial sea squirts are soft and slippery, while the encrusting sponges are rougher and often crumble like wet bread when rubbed. Sea anemones feel different from sea cucumbers, even though they look much alike when strongly contracted. So don't be afraid of *gently* touching most creatures that you see on our Northwest seashores.

3

What makes a beach?

Obviously, a beach occurs when land meets sea. Beyond this simple statement, however, things get complicated rapidly, even before adding plants and animals to the situation. Three major factors control most of this complexity: (1) the material composing the beach (rock, gravel, sand, mud, clay), (2) the effect of waves and currents on the beach (from the outer coast, exposed to the full force of ocean storms to the innermost, protected bays), and (3) the duration that any level of beach is out of the water during low tide and exposed to sun, heat, freezing, drying, and predation from land animals, including man. The great number of possible combinations among these physical and biological factors leads to an almost infinite variety of beaches. It remains a major challenge for seashore ecologists to understand and explain the ways by which organisms adapt to their ever-changing environments. Knowledge of the kinds of beaches is an important base for understanding the plants and animals that live there.

Rocky Beaches

The classical rocky beach is composed of solid, immovable bedrock to which plants and animals can attach without any possibility that their home will be moved around or turned over by the waves from a winter storm. The size of an immovable object is therefore relative to the size of the waves that can occur at that location. A ten-ton boulder on a fully exposed ocean beach may be a very insecure dwelling place, while a ten-pound cobblestone at the

19

back of a quiet bay in southern Puget Sound may not move for many years. Thus, the size of rocks found on beaches classified as rocky overlaps with the size of those found on beaches classified as gravel, depending on their degree of protection from wave action. Big waves may keep some pretty large rocks barren by rolling them over during storms and crushing everything on the surface. In other cases, some stable rocks that rest on sand or small gravel may have growth on the top, but have the bottom fringes polished clean by wave-carried sand and gravel.

The greatest numbers of individuals and species are found on stable rocky beaches, regardless of the amount of wave action. On exposed rocky beaches, many species are so well adapted to resisting the constant pounding of the waves that they have become "addicted" to the high levels of oxygen that occur in the surf and are unable to live anywhere else.

With continued wave action, large rocks are broken into smaller rocks and eventually into gravel of decreasing size. If the wave action is sufficiently strong, the smaller rocks are carried out into deeper water, rather than accumulating on the beach. Thus a really exposed rocky beach has little loose material on it. See Figures 11-78 for the animals found on rocky beaches.

Gravel Beaches

Where wave action is strong, gravel beaches are usually barren. Few, if any, animals can survive the tumbling action of constantly moving rocks. In protected waters, on the other hand, gravel mixed with a little sand or mud provides a relatively loose mixture wherein clams and other animals can burrow easily. Therefore, many of the more protected gravel beaches of Puget Sound are clam digging areas, and in general, animals are found *in* the beach, rather than *on* it. Seaweeds are also abundant here, but as they grow larger, some become increasingly buoyant and float away, dragging or carrying their rock anchors if they have chosen too small a stone on which to grow.

Gravel is eventually pulverized into sand, which strong wave action carries either into deeper water or laterally along the beach. Apparently stable sand beaches on the outer coast are dependent upon a continuing source of sand. The Columbia River, for example, supplies much of the sand of the beaches along either side of its mouth. Sand in quantities necessary to maintain these beaches does not come from grinding of gravel on the beach — it was preground by rivers and glaciers. Figures 79-95 show the animals found on gravel beaches.

Sandy Beaches

Many people visualize a surf-pounded sandy beach as the typical ocean seashore — rows of waves breaking and rolling up onto great expanses of flat sand. With the exception of a handful of species, however, this environment

20

is an impossible habitat for seashore creatures. The sand is always moving, unstable. Because the major protection is under the sand, species that excel at survival also excel at digging. The razor clam is a good example of a successful inhabitant of this difficult environment, where the roof moves a little with every wave, where it may change several feet during a single tidal cycle, and may be completely renovated during a storm. Further, there is not much to eat on a sandy beach, so most species must maintain a connection to the water above in order to feed on plankton or on the finely ground debris and bacteria which make up the brown scum at the water's edge.

Sandy beaches in protected areas are not too different from exposed ones except in the greater number of inhabitants. Here, too, most residents burrow for protection, but the digging needn't be so frantic or constant. A more common problem is making a burrow in soft sand stable enough not to require constant repair. Living in soft sand can also be a defense of sorts, because it makes the animal difficult to capture — the hole you dig to capture it collapses before you can find the animal, as any digger of gweducs (usually pronounced "gooey-ducks") can tell you.

It is not commonly known that even protected sandy beaches need a supply of sand to remain stable. The rate at which new sand is needed depends on how rapidly waves and currents carry it away, usually out to deeper water. Marine engineers are now beginning to understand the dynamics of some of these rivers of sand and mud and why dredged channels, breakwaters, and other man-made structures that interfere with their flow sometimes cause unexpected excavations or depositions of sand. You are seeing some of this sand transport occur when you notice areas of surf that appear dirty rather than white or long tongues of dirty floodwater extending out into the sea from the mouths of rivers; the dirty color is produced by sand as it travels seaward. See Figures 96-125 for sandy beach animals.

Mud Beaches

Mud beaches exist only in the most protected waters — if there were a lot of current or wave action, the mud would not have settled there in the first place. Mud also forms mixtures with sand and gravel so that some mud beaches are firm enough to walk on easily, while others are almost thin enough to swim in. Mud beaches contain much decomposing organic matter and bacteria, which is why these beaches sometimes have a bad odor. The combination of bacteria and mud serves as a bountiful food supply for some animals, but for others, it is a suffocating blanket which clogs gills and makes locomotion a struggle. The most successful inhabitants are a few specialized clams and a whole array of burrowing worms.

Quiet waters in the vicinity of mud beaches are also often nutritious,

21

producing thick, green plankton blooms which are excellent places to grow oysters. However, oysters suffocate if allowed to sink into the mud, so oyster growers "harden" their oyster beds by adding gravel. In some rather soft areas, oystermen wear a kind of snowshoe for walking on their oyster grounds. Consequently, oyster beds built on mud beaches represent considerable labor and investment — $1,000 an acre or more. Oysters, of course, can also grow on protected gravel and rocky beaches. While oyster dikes in muddy areas represent an artificial environment, the animals don't care and an interesting assemblage of species lives there. See Figures 126-127 for inhabitants of sandy mud, Figures 128-137 for mud beach animals.

Clay Beaches

Clay beaches are mostly a curious combination of a mud beach and rocky beach, with most of the bad features of each. Clay is too hard to penetrate for most animals that might burrow in sand or mud, but it is usually not firm enough to allow barnacles, mussels, seaweeds, and other sessile (permanently attached) life to take hold. Thus, it is a fairly sterile environment, except for the piddocks (Figure 75) and other boring clams that can survive there. The abandoned holes of piddocks might be expected to house about the same assemblage of creatures as are found in holes and crevices on a rocky beach except that the beach stability is poor — a projecting ledge of clay with one-inch diameter piddock holes bored through it falls apart rather quickly — so the population density is low.

Neither are clay beaches very common. The description above is based on only three examples that I know of in Puget Sound in Washington. One is on the west side of Port Washington Narrows separating East Bremerton from Bremerton and leading into Dyes Inlet. Another is at the tip of Point Defiance Park at the north entrance of the Tacoma Narrows. The third includes both shores of the long, narrow channel (Hammersley Inlet) leading into Oakland Bay at Shelton. All three are characterized by moderately fast tidal flow. There may be other localized outcroppings of clay unknown to me, but this type of beach will not be discussed further because of its limited occurrence and restricted life.

Man-made Beaches – Breakwaters, Piling, Floats

If a man-made surface is solid and not toxic — rock fill and concrete, old car bodies and tires — plants and animals attach to the surface just as they would to natural rock. Floats, on the other hand, are a very special environment. While they are near the surface and readily accessible to view anytime, they are never exposed to the air unless someone takes them out of the water. Also, floats are independent from both the shore and the bottom, so the inhabitants avoid at least some of their ordinary predators. Because floats are usually in protected areas, many of the species there also grow

22

more ornately and luxuriantly than in any other place.

Floats are fascinating to study, both for what you can see there and for trying to figure out why some forms of life occur there and others do not. See Figures 138-148 for examples of animals on floats.

Exposed versus Protected Beaches

A completely exposed beach has no protection from the full force of the open sea — no offshore reefs, islands, or even kelp beds. Certain species, such as the sea palm and the goose barnacle, are found only under these strenuous conditions. Some marine biologists distinguish minor differences among slightly different degrees of extreme exposure, but for general purposes all of the ocean beaches of Oregon, Washington, and Vancouver Island can be classified as exposed (see map).

It takes only minor geographical differences to change the degree of exposure significantly. Since most winter storms in this area come from the south, beaches that face north are partially protected. In traveling only four or five miles from Cape Flattery, Washington, eastward to Neah Bay, there are noticeable changes in the intertidal ecology; these north-facing beaches are increasingly protected even farther eastward. On the British Columbia side of the Strait of Juan de Fuca, beaches face the southerly storms, so species typical of the exposed coast are found much farther east — sixty miles or more. Similar distributions of species are found on the north and south shores of Barkley Sound on Vancouver Island for the same geographical reasons.

Protected beaches also occur in many degrees. The eastern portions of the Strait of Juan de Fuca can be nearly as violent at times as the open sea (at least it seems so to skippers of small boats), but many animals found on the exposed coast are absent there. Therefore, the inner parts of the Strait and outer parts of the San Juan Islands are labeled "transitional" on the map. Once inside Puget Sound, Hood Canal, or the San Juan or Canadian Gulf islands, there are still greater degrees of protection. Wave action is much less, and tidal currents may become significant in ways not found in more open waters. Sand and gravel bluffs, which would not survive long in the presence of the outer coast's surf, tower above many protected beaches. Even then, portions of these bluffs slide down onto the beach during the heavy winter rains, endangering property owners who built houses too close to the edge above and killing the beach animals covered by the slide, but at the same time resupplying the beach with sand and gravel. There are as many degrees of protected beaches as there are degrees of exposed beaches, although the protected variations are not as spectacular as their counterparts on the outer coast.

4

Rocky beaches

Exposed and Transitional Rocky Beaches – Examples and Species

Cape Flattery is the northwesternmost point of the contiguous United States and is reached by a trail about one mile long from a road on the Makah Indian Reservation. While there is no beach there in the usual sense, if you peek over the edge, the intertidal zone and its plants and animals are still visible on the vertical face of the rocks.

Surf pounding the north jetty at Westport, Washington, on an average day (when you might be able to get close to it) gives some idea of what permanent residents on these rocks have to withstand. This is a dangerous place for people anytime, but is inhabited by the same plants and animals that live on natural rocks.

The Olympic Strip (Olympic National Park) has alternating rocky headlands and sandy/gravel beaches. Cape Alava is the strip's best-known point and is the site of an archeological excavation which is accessible by trail from the town of Ozette. Small rivers along the Olympic Strip beaches break through the sand dunes and carry sand out onto what might otherwise have been fairly rocky beaches. Where there is a mixture of sand and rock, typical of many coastal beaches in Washington, the scouring action of the sand prevents much from growing on the smaller rocks and lower parts of the larger ones.

Rocky, *Exposed*

11. Rocky point near La Push, Wa.

Figure 11: Close-up of a rocky point near La Push shows the isolated pillars and piles of large rubble in front of the point, which probably represents the location of the point a few hundred thousand years ago.

Figure 12: Rocky beaches on the Strait of Juan de Fuca between Neah Bay and Sekiu, Washington, have steeply tilted rock layers of differing hardness with a layer of boulders on top. This often leads to the formation of many cracks, crevices, and tide pools where a number of species prefer to live. There is almost no surf during the summer, and the beach is also somewhat protected in winter because it faces north. During storms the Strait can get very rough. The beach is defined as having a transitional degree of exposure.

A bit farther east, the rocky point at the east end of Clallam Bay, usually accessible through the Coast Guard station, is a solid rock headland facing westward, which gets considerable surf at times. It has a richly varied fauna and flora, but a few extreme coastal species are lacking. Thus, it is a transitional beach.

Figure 13: A view of a transitional rocky beach on Barkley Sound, west of Bamfield, British Columbia, shows typical amounts of brown rockweed on top of the mid-tide rocks. The closeness of trees to the high tide line of this north-facing beach indicates a lesser degree of wave action than is found on exposed beaches facing west only two to three miles away. Comparable conditions occur along the south shore of the Strait of Juan de Fuca.

26

12. Rocky beach between Neah Bay and Sekiu, Wa.

13. Brown rockweed on transitional rocky beach, Barkley Sound, B.C.

Lynwood S. Smith

Rocky, *Exposed*

14. Sea louse *(Ligia pallasii)*

Figure 14: The sea louse *(Ligia pallasii)* of the outer coast is neutral gray in color and inhabits caves, crevices, and other dark places near or even above the high tide line. Up to one inch long, it scuttles about rapidly and feeds on debris.

Figure 15: This brown seaweed, the sea palm, grows on solid rocks that are just barely covered at high tide. Like a miniature palm tree, it stands up to eighteen inches high, hence the name *Postelsia palmaeformis.* It is much more flexible and tougher than a tree, however, and seems to thrive on the pounding surf. This seaweed occurs only on the most exposed beaches and not at all on the transitional beaches.

Figure 16: Goose barnacles *(Pollicipes polymerus)* are found high on the beach growing in clusters on exposed rocks. They stand on tough, resilient stalks; the white plates cover a set of rake-shaped feet which pop out to feed on passing debris as a wave hits.

28

15. Sea palm *(Postelsia palmaeformis)*

16. Goose barnacles *(Pollicipes polymerus)*

29

Rocky, *Exposed*

17. Ribbed barnacles *(Balanus crenatus)* and California mussels *(Mytilus californianus)*

Figure 17: Barnacles and mussels — here *Balanus crenatus,* the ribbed barnacle (white), and *Mytilus californianus,* the California mussel (blue) — are the basis for a major community on the higher part of the beach. When they are very high on the beach, the groupings are relatively small, as here; lower down, they form a nearly solid mat. This common mussel of the outer coast has a ribbed rather than smooth shell (as in the bay mussel) and grows six to eight inches long at low levels on the beach. Commonly associated animals include periwinkle snails (Figure 47) and limpets (Figure 19, also known as Chinese hat shells), both seen as fairly small specimens in this picture.

30

18. Rough green sea anemones *(Anthopleura elegantissima)*

Figure 18: A little farther down the beach, the barnacle/mussel community is joined by larger limpets (see Figure 19) and rough green sea anemones. To resist drying out during low tide, anemones often cluster in crevices and may also coat themselves with shell fragments. These anemones *(Anthopleura elegantissima)* are found on a variety of beaches and exposures. They are distinguished by sticky lumps on the sides of their bodies and when expanded, by a faintly purplish hue on their tentacles' tips. The anemones are important scavengers, eating large quantities of both plant and animal debris that washes up on the beach.

Rocky, *Exposed*

19. Plate limpet *(Notoacmea scutum)*

20. Green sea anemones *(Anthopleura xanthogrammica)*

Figure 19: The plate limpet *(Notoacmea scutum)* is one of the common limpets. It is distinguished by a somewhat rounded shape, eccentric peak, and radiating lines of color. The identification of limpets has been changed several times in the last fifty years because of the great variability in shape within a species. Hybridization among some species has been suggested to account for the many grades of these variations.

Limpets of several sizes and species can be seen in many of the pictures showing rocks. There are several other species of *Notoacmea* and even more species of another genus, *Collisella,* which are relatively common and require some practice with a technical key or detailed pictures to identify.

Figure 20: This large green sea anemone *(Anthopleura xanthogrammica)* is characteristic of tide pools along the low tide line. It is usually solitary (does not touch another) and preys on small animals that blunder into its stinging tentacles. Large specimens can be six to eight inches in diameter. It is distinguished by being green all over, including the tips of the tentacles, and by being found on exposed and transitional beaches, but not protected ones.

Figure 21: Brown rockweed *(Fucus)* is a reliable indicator of the mid-tide zone. It branches out into fronds a foot or more long and, when mature, has "bulbs" with two "ears" that pop when squeezed. It is common on rocky beaches from the most exposed outer coast to sheltered parts of Puget Sound. Beside the rockweed are contracted anemones (upper right) which were shown expanded in Figure 18.

21. Brown rockweed *(Fucus)*

33

Rocky, *Exposed*

Figure 22: Tucked away in many of the nooks and crannies and under the seaweeds of the middle intertidal zone is this pretty little hermit crab *(Pagurus samuelis).* Hermit crabs are scavengers in two ways — they clean up many dead and decaying organisms, and they use empty snail shells as protection for their soft abdomens. Their agility in scampering about in tide pools is great fun to watch and the speed with which they can withdraw into their snail shells is almost too fast to see. Turn one of the snail shells with the opening upwards after the crab has withdrawn into its shell and watch its greatly varied motions in righting itself and general versatility in getting around, both in and out of the water.

Figure 23: Where major food resources such as masses of mussels and barnacles are found, predators such as starfish are rarely far away. Most conspicuous among starfish of the outer coast are these heavy-bodied purple (ochre) stars *(Pisaster ochraceus),* which are typically found along the lower edges of mussel beds and can be purple, orange, or chocolate brown in color. They attach firmly to the rocks with their tube feet and rarely move while exposed, but easily pull open barnacles and mussels when underwater. Clustering may reduce drying during exposure to air.

Figure 24: The six-rayed or brooding starfish *(Leptasterias hexactis)* is common on outer, transitional, and more open protected beaches, usually on the undersides of rocks or sometimes in protected crevices. Typically gray, there are color variations from splotchy cream and lavender to almost black. It is the only starfish that consistently has six arms; most others have five or multiples of five, except the large sunflower star (Figure 111). Also, this is the only local starfish that humps up and retains its eggs beneath its body until they become miniature adults. All other starfish have free-swimming larval stages.

Chitons (kitons) are similar to snails but have eight separate shells, each shaped somewhat like a butterfly, instead of a single shell. The shell of the leather or black chiton *(Katharina tunicata)* is nearly covered by the mantle (the flesh next to the shell), which feels like wet leather, and only a small, diamond-shaped portion of each shell is seen outside. The eight shells are held together with strong muscles and ligaments, and the broad foot can hang on to rocks firmly, so chitons are very resistant to wave damage. Chitons eat algae and reside in the lower intertidal zones, often making an open space in an otherwise luxuriant mat of seaweed. Leather chitons are also found on transitional rocky beaches. (Photo also shows several large barnacles.)

hermit crab, starfish, chiton

22. Hermit crab *(Pagurus samuelis)*

23. Purple (ochre) stars *(Pisaster ochraceus)*

24. Six-rayed starfish
    (Leptasterias hexactis)
    and leather chiton
    (Katharina tunicata)

Rocky, *Exposed*

27. Brittle or serpent star *(Ophiopholis aculeata)*

25. Blood star *(Henricia leviuscula)*

26. Broad disc star *(Mediaster aequalis)*

Figure 25: The blood star *(Henricia leviuscula)* is found in lower tide pools and is always conspicuous, although not always red. The round, slim arms and firm body have led to its common exploitation as a tourist memento, which is a poor idea, since the species is not really abundant.

Figure 26: The broad disc star *(Mediaster aequalis)* might be confused with the blood star (Figure 25) because of its bright red color and because it is found in similar places. However, its center is wider and flatter than the blood star's and there is a distinctive row of plates along the sides of each arm. The tube feet are extended beneath one arm and are distinctly visible in the picture.

Figure 27: Brittle or serpent stars *(Ophiopholis aculeata)* are quite different from any of the starfish above and derive their name from their fragile arms. The body is distinctively separate from the arms, which are highly flexible and mobile even when brittle stars are out of water. They commonly live in crevices or under rocks (except rocks on mud or sand). When living in piddock holes in solid rock, two or three arms may extend out of the hole (presumably for feeding purposes), giving the appearance of brightly colored, miniature fern fronds. While the name serpent star suggests a slithering motion, they more often "walk" with one arm in front, two arms moving somewhat in breaststroke fashion, and two arms trailing. A few specimens have been seen doing this rapidly enough to swim. This species occurs only on exposed and transitional beaches. A drabber species (not illustrated) that has much longer, thinner arms occurs in Puget Sound on gravel under protected rocks (see also Figure 62).

Rocky, *Exposed*

Figure 28: In mid-level tide pools of the outer coast and even on rather exposed bare rock, you will find large numbers of the stubby black turban snail *(Tegula funebralis)*, almost always with a white patch on the end where the spire of the shell has been worn away. A green isopod (Figure 56) is immediately below the turban snail. Also shown are several species of other snails. The most conspicuous one is the common whelk *(Thais emarginata)*, seen on either side of the black turban.

Figure 29: The abalone *(Haliotis kamtschatkana)* is one of the larger snails of the Pacific Northwest, mostly inhabiting the outer coasts and feeding on large algae (kelp). While larger, older specimens are well camouflaged, the younger ones are brightly colored and conspicuous. Regardless of size, they cling tightly to rocks with their broad, muscular foot. You usually need to visit remote beaches to find them, as they are popularly taken as food. They are also more numerous subtidally than intertidally. Both size and number are regulated by government agencies of the area, so check local sport fishing regulations before taking any.

Figure 30: The underside of an abalone is no less spectacular than the upper side. There are fleshy flaps (mantle) alongside the foot (the part sought by predators), which are mottled with many colors. When loosened from the substrate and turned upside down, the abalone can extend these flaps completely over its foot, as shown in the photo, to protect this delicious piece of meat.

snail, abalone

28. Turban snail *(Tegula funebralis)*
and whelks *(Thais emarginata)*

29. Abalone
(Haliotis kamtschatkana)

30. Abalone, underside

Rocky, *Exposed*

31. Keyhole limpet
(*Diodora aspera*)

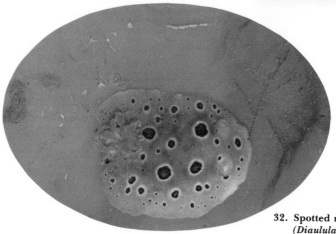

32. Spotted nudibranch
(*Diaulula sandiegensis*)

33. Red nudibranch (*Rostanga pulchra*) on red sponge (*Ophlitaspongia pennata*)

snail, worm, nudibranch

Figure 31: The keyhole limpet *(Diodora aspera)* is larger and taller than most other limpets on the outer coast and is readily distinguished from others by the hole at the apex of the shell. It grazes on algae and is found at the lowest tide levels. If you carefully pry the limpet away from the rock by inserting a putty knife or similar tool underneath it, you can often find a scale worm *(Arctonoë vittata)* tucked in between the foot and the mantle, a nicely protected habitat. It does not harm the limpet, but no one seems to know what the worm eats or does.

Figure 32: Nudibranchs are a group of snails that lack shells; their name means "bare gills." The type pictured, called a dorid nudibranch (see also Figure 69), withdraws its gills into a cavity around the anal opening when exposed to air or when disturbed. The spotted nudibranch *(Diaulula sandiegensis)* seen here is commonly found singly, feeding on sponge except when mating.

Figure 33: This bright red nudibranch *(Rostanga pulchra)* is a small dorid nudibranch (see Figures 32, 69). It is easily overlooked because it feeds on a bright red sponge *(Ophlitaspongia pennata)* which occurs in large, gaudy patches. This nudibranch is usually found on or close to the sponge in the lower tide zone. The spiral below the nudibranch is a mass of its eggs, also red.

41

Rocky, *Exposed*

Figure 34: The mossy chiton *(Mopalia muscosa)* and two other similar species expose a somewhat larger proportion of each of their shells than the leather chiton (Figure 24). The mantle around the edge of the shells is "mossy." Part of this fuzz is produced by the chiton; part may be algae. Mossy chitons can be found on all kinds of rocky beaches in the lower levels.

Figure 35: The lined chiton *(Tonicella lineata)* is typically a little smaller than most of the other chitons, has characteristic bright stripes, but is quite variable in color — orange, red, green, and mixtures.

Figure 36: The moccasin chiton *(Cryptochiton stelleri)* is our largest chiton, but it is unspectacular otherwise. It is colored an earthy brown, and the shells are completely covered by the mantle, although bulges in the animal's outline may show its position. The moccasin chiton is also called the gum boot because it is about the size of a rubber shoe and has about the same edibility. This species occurs on all rocky beaches where there is a lot of solid rock.

42

34. Mossy chiton *(Mopalia muscosa)*   35. Lined chiton *(Tonicella lineata)*

36. Moccasin chiton *(Cryptochiton stelleri)*

Rocky, *Exposed*

Figure 37: This shows the underside of the moccasin chiton in Figure 36. In the middle is the broad foot, with the head showing as a slightly separated area at the right end of the foot. The gills are in a groove on either side of the foot. On the side, the broad strip of flexible mantle helps the chiton conform to the rocks underneath. Although the foot is large and looks potentially edible, it is really very tough.

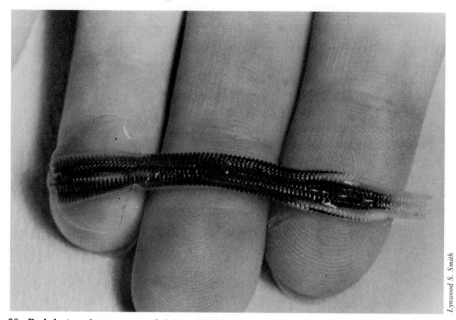

Lynwood S. Smith

38. **Radula (rasping tongue) of the mocassin chiton**

Figure 38: Inside the head of every chiton is a rasping tongue (radula) with which it eats seaweed and scrapes algal slime off the rocks. Snails also have the same structure; some use it for boring holes in clamshells. This is the radula from a large moccasin chiton; those from other chitons and snails are in proportion to their size. Octopus and squid also have a radula in addition to their parrotlike beak.

Figure 39: When an encrusting layer looks and feels like stiff gelatin, especially if moderately thick and fairly brightly colored, it is probably a colonial tunicate (also called compound ascidian). Upon careful examination, you should also see subunits spaced throughout the mass, each with its own opening to the surface. These openings are usually closed when out of water. Each animal filters food from the water, but also shares its food with the rest of the colony via a common gut. The identification of species in this group is difficult without dissecting out individuals under magnification.

44

37. Moccasin chiton, underside

39. Colonial tunicate

Rocky, *Exposed*

40. Bread crumb sponge

41. Purple urchins *(Strongylocentrotus purpuratus)*

Figure 40: In contrast to the patches of colonial tunicates which never get very large or very thick — a few square inches in area and one-fourth inch thick — some of the sponges get large enough to fill a small dishpan. There are many varieties and colors, most of which have to be identified by dissolving the animal material and looking at the spiny internal structure, often made of lime or silica. The shapes of the sponges tend to follow the substrate, but with irregular bulges and large openings for water to flow out. The water from which they filter their food flows in through very tiny pores all over the surface of the sponge. Also in contrast to colonial tunicates, these sponges are not firm and slippery, but more like worn-out bath sponge which crumbles when it is handled. Because of the difficulty in identifying sponges, a variety of common names have sprung up which describe their general appearance — bread crumb sponge being a commonly heard name for thickly encrusting sponges (see also Figure 146). A thinly encrusting sponge is shown in Figure 57.

Figure 41: Purple urchins *(Strongylocentrotus purpuratus)* inhabit extensive areas of rocky coastline near and below the low tide line. In more protected areas of the outer and transitional coast, they may be on open rock but in more exposed areas they are often in custom-fitted holes in the solid rocks. They do not occur on protected rocky beaches. The spines of these sea urchins are in constant motion and may wear the holes into the rock, or perhaps some kind of secretion dissolves the rock. Sea urchins also have tube feet like starfish and use them both for hanging on to rock and for walking, in combination with the spines. Urchins eat seaweed and in turn are eaten by sea otters and people, the gonads being the main edible part. Taking of sea urchins is now regulated in some areas — check your local sport fishing regulations (see also Figure 76).

Rocky, *Exposed*

43. Clingfish *(Gobiesox maeandricus)*

44. Clingfish, underside

42. Porcelain crab *(Petrolisthes eriomerus)*

Figure 42: The porcelain crab *(Petrolisthes eriomerus)* is small, flat, and one of the faster-moving creatures on rocky seashores. The name comes from its fragility, and its thin shape is ideal for moving about under rocks and in crevices. It has special mechanisms for cutting loose legs that get trapped in tight places and can grow new legs during subsequent molts. If comparing this with other crabs, note that it has one less pair of walking legs than usual — the last pair is nonfunctional and tucked in close to the body over the hindmost pair of functional legs. Porcelain crabs occur on the most rocky beaches in the low tide zone.

Figure 43: The clingfish *(Gobiesox maeandricus)* occurs in tide pools and under rocks from the outer coast to the more exposed beaches of Puget Sound. It has a broad, flattened head with a sucker on the underside (see Figure 44) that is formed by specially shaped pectoral fins and is obviously useful for holding on in its environment during wave surges. Wet your hands before handling the fish; then you can pick it up and observe its suction on your hand.

Figure 44: By turning the clingfish over (using wet hands so as not to damage its mucus layer and possibly cause the fish to become infected later), you can readily see the size and extent of the sucker and the pectoral fins which help form it. Test the suction by letting the fish attach to the palm of your hand and then turning your hand over — the fish more than supports its own weight. On the other hand, the suction disc will not work on rough surfaces, so clingfish are found only on beaches with relatively smooth rocks.

Rocky, *Protected*

Protected Rocky Beaches – Examples and Species

The south shore of Sucia Island State Park, Washington, is hardly a calm or protected beach, especially during winter storms. However, it lacks a number of species characteristic of the exposed rocky coast and must be classified in our scheme as a protected beach. Fossil Bay, a protected, popular anchorage for yachtsmen on the southeastern shore of the island, has a mud bottom, another characteristic not found on the outer coast. At the water's edge there is a luxuriant growth of kelp. Many of the other rocky San Juan Islands facing moderate stretches of open water have similar beaches. Most bays and inner islands are more protected, similar to Fossil Bay, with solid and broken rocks on the upper beach and a tidal zone composed of sandy mud or mud.

Figure 45: Among the rockier protected beaches of Puget Sound is a portion of Alki Beach, just south of the lighthouse at the south point of Elliott Bay, Seattle. Some of this rock is in solid ridges; other rock varies from huge boulders to sandy gravel. The beach is stable enough to be highly productive for many species of plants and animals.

Nearly half the rocks in this picture are barren because they are upside down. Even on a fairly protected beach, rocks of this size are a marginal place to live because they can be tumbled around during severe storms. Then, when abuse by people is also added, the results can be environmentally disastrous.

45. Protected rocky beach, Alki Beach, Seattle, Wa.

46. Seaweed-covered boulder on Alki Beach

Figure 46: Boulders at the low tide line show most of the major types of large seaweed. The filmy material (green) on top of the rock is sea lettuce *(Ulva)*. The strands with a bulb and smooth leaves on the end (brown), hanging from the boulder and on the smaller rock, are bladder or seal head kelp *(Nereocystis)*, which children use for whips. It is also found just offshore with the handle end of the "whip" floating at the surface. The wavy (brown) sheet of algae, on the lower portion of the smaller rock, is typical of several species generally classed under the name *Laminaria;* most have fairly short stems and a single broad blade. In the water with many tiny floats is another (brown) alga, *Sargassum,* which is characteristic of many protected Puget Sound beaches. Most seaweeds, large and small, are seasonal; they grow for one season, reproduce, and die off each winter.

Further north in Puget Sound, Camano Island State Park has a predominantly rocky beach along the north half of the park, below the northern parking lot. The beach is composed of gravel at the high tide line, small boulders at the low tide line. Rocks at this beach are much smaller than those at Alki. They are covered only with sea lettuce and are much more restricted

Rocky, *Protected*

in species diversity than those at Alki. Camano represents a fairly typical rocky beach in Puget Sound.

The north portion of Golden Gardens beach in Seattle is a marginally rocky beach. It has one large stable boulder and a number of smaller rocks that rest on sandy gravel. The lower portion of the beach is mostly sand with some eelgrass, small kelp, and a few tide pools. Farther south, the beach is barren gravel or sand.

Figure 47: The highest tide zone on protected rocks is much like the outer coast — a very difficult place to live. Common inhabitants here are acorn barnacles (*Balanus,* right, bottom, and left edge), limpets (here *Collisella digitalis,* upper left) and littorine (periwinkle) snails (*Littorina,* center). All three types of animals are much smaller than on the outer coast and are different species. The largest of the littorine snails in the picture is about the size of a dime, while a related species (not shown) is about the size of a pea.

Figure 48: About the middle of the beach and on the sides of the rocks one frequently finds wrinkled purple snails *(Thais lamellosa),* which are a kind of whelk. In season, you may also find grainlike egg cases, sometimes mistaken for separate organisms. The snails and egg cases may occur in great clusters. When newly formed, the egg cases are light in color and pinhead-sized pink embryos can be seen moving around inside. The juvenile whelks emerge from their egg cases by cutting off the tip of the case and crawling away as miniature adults.

47. Acorn barnacles, limpets, and littorine snails

48. Wrinkled purple snails *(Thais lamellosa)* **and eggs**

Rocky, *Protected*

50. Mottled starfish
(Evasterias troschelii)
and eggs of sea lemon
(Anisodoris nobilis)

49. Rockweed community at Alki Beach, Seattle, Wa.

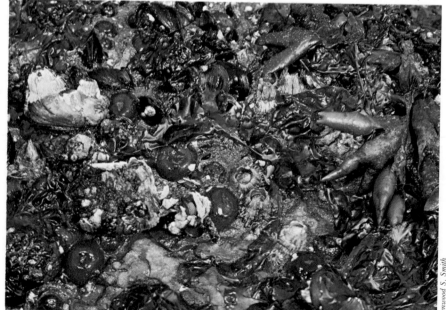

Lynwood S. Smith

54

Figure 49: The rough green anemone extends down the beach to the upper extent of the green sea lettuce and to the lower extent of the brown rockweed. A bay mussel *(Mytilus edulis)* and some ribbed barnacles *(Balanus cariosus),* which grow larger as they occur lower on the beach, are also visible in this figure.

Figure 50: Generally found either under or beside rocks, the most common starfish is the mottled star, which comes in a variety of muted colors — blue, gray, orange, reddish, and soft brown. The arms are more slender and the central disc is smaller in proportion to total size than in the coastal starfish. In spite of the color variation, all of these starfish are the same species, *Evasterias troschelii.* They behave like ordinary starfish: they scavenge and eat barnacles, mussels, and other bivalves.

The yellowish sheet of material attached to the rock is a mass of eggs produced by the nudibranch *Anisodoris nobilis,* one of the sea lemons (see also Figures 32, 33, 69, 72).

Rocky, *Protected*

Figure 51: The leather star *(Dermasterias imbricata)* earns its name because out of water it looks and feels like smooth, wet leather. Underwater, it may appear quite fuzzy because the skin gills (found in all starfish) are not surrounded by the spines found in most starfish species. Its color is a pleasingly mottled mixture of earthy reds, brown, greens, and even some purple. A pea-sized white disc (yellowish in this photo), just off-center, is the filtered intake port for the hydraulic system that operates the tube feet on the underside of each arm. Sometimes found on gravel and shell bottoms, leather stars seem to prefer the sides and tops of rocks above tide pools, in well-protected areas with good water circulation. They are also found subtidally.

Figure 52: Another conspicuous inhabitant of solid rocks lives in shiny white, irregularly coiled tubes. The worm inside this tube hardens it with lime, making the tube larger and longer as the worm grows. On its head, the worm wears feathery tentacles and a funnel-shaped organ, both of which are bright red and white. The worm is very sensitive and withdraws suddenly with any unusual disturbance. Its common name, serpulid worm, or calcareous tube worm, is taken from the scientific name, *Serpula vermicularis.* It feeds by filtering small particles out of the water around it.

52. Calcareous tube worm *(Serpula vermicularis)*

51. Leather star
(Dermasterias imbricata)

Rocky, *Protected*

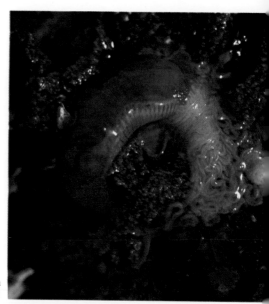

53. Shellbinder worm
(Thelepus crispus)

54. Ribbon or nemertean worm

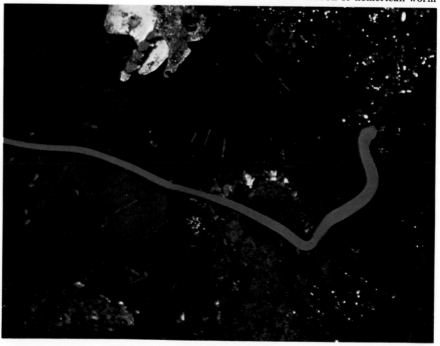

Figure 53: Another worm found strictly under or between rocks is the shellbinder worm *(Thelepus crispus)*. It builds a fragile tube out of mud and mucus and has no bright color except for a small tuft of blood red respiratory tentacles (these tentacles have hemoglobin in their blood). The remainder of the tentacles are long, thin, white, and contractile, and each has a ciliated groove which brings food particles to the mouth. There seems to be no basis for the name shellbinder, since the tentacles are quite fragile and could not bind anything.

Figure 54: Although the word *worm* leaves a bad taste with some people, the nemertean or ribbon worm does not have the appearance that accompanies that connotation. Many are spectacularly colored — bright red, bright green, solid or with contrasting stripes. A few are drab brown or brownish gray. They can stretch to two feet or more in length and are so stretchable that it is difficult to know what their "normal" length really is. These worms are quite fragile and easily broken if stretched excessively, and since they are often wound around seaweed holdfasts, barnacles, mussels, etc., it can be difficult to obtain an entire worm. They are distinguished from most other worms by being unsegmented — just a simple ribbon of smooth muscle that encloses a simple digestive tube.

There are about two dozen species of ribbon worms in the Puget Sound region, which require a detailed key for identification.

Rocky, *Protected*

Figure 55: Flatworms *(Freemania litoricola)* are easy to overlook. They are colored a mottled drab gray and brown, are rarely over three-fourths inch long, and generally look like slimy pieces of debris. Nudge them gently with your finger, however, and they flow with apparent effortlessness over and around the barnacles on the underside of mid-tide-level rocks. They probably scavenge and feed on barnacles.

Figure 56: Another occupant of the sides and undersides of rocks is a distant cousin of the terrestrial sow bug. The green sea louse *(Idotea wosnesenskii)* is an isopod, most commonly olive green in color, which feeds mostly on plant debris. It is a surprisingly good swimmer and can cling tightly to rocks, barnacles, eelgrass, or even your finger with seven pairs of legs shaped like the ice tongs used to carry blocks of ice.

Figure 57: An encrusting sponge is generally found among the various encrustations on the undersides of rocks. It has irregular miniature "volcanoes" on its surface through which filtered water is exhaled (the water comes in through a great many tiny pores) and may also have channels running along its surface. Most sponges feel somewhat gritty to the touch and may crumble like old sponge rubber. This is in contrast to colonial tunicates (Figure 39), which are firm and slick, or to coralline algae (Figure 67), which are hard and rough like plaster.

worm, sea louse, sponge

55. Flatworm *(Freemania litoricola)*

56. Green sea louses *(Idotea wosnesenskii)*

57. Encrusting sponge

61

Rocky, *Protected*

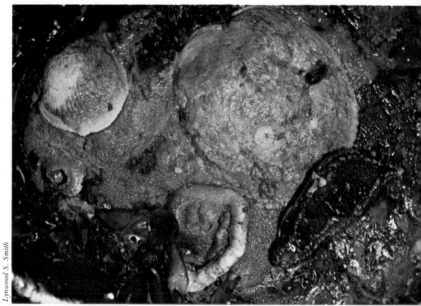

Lynwood S. Smith

58. Rock oysters *(Pododesmus macroschisma)*, calcareous tube worm, and orange sea cucumber

59. Orange sea cucumber *(Cucumaria miniata)*

Figure 58: The rock oyster or jingle shell *(Pododesmus macroschisma)*, a bivalve resembling a limpet at first glance, is permanently attached to the rock. The muscle, which in oysters holds the shells closed, passes through the shell next to the rock and attaches directly to the rock. Unlike a chiton or a snail, the jingle shell cannot reattach itself once removed from a rock. Also pictured, besides the two rock oysters, are a calcareous tube worm (Figure 52) and an orange sea cucumber, strongly contracted and attached to the rock by its tube feet as you would typically find it out of water (see Figure 59).

Figure 59: The orange sea cucumber *(Cucumaria miniata)*, a relative of the starfish, has five rows of tube feet and, when expanded underwater, a set of finely divided tentacles with which it filters food out of the water. Look for expanded cucumbers in tide pools and along the low tide line.

Figure 60: Another smaller cucumber is white and similar in habits and habitat to the orange sea cucumber (Figure 59). The white sea cucumber *(Eupentacta pseudoquinquesemita)*, however, may hold on to pieces of seaweed or shell with its tube feet, perhaps for camouflage. A related species, *E. quinquesemita,* is cream-colored or off-white with purple, black, or brown speckles.

60. White sea cucumber *(Eupentacta pseudoquinquesemita)*

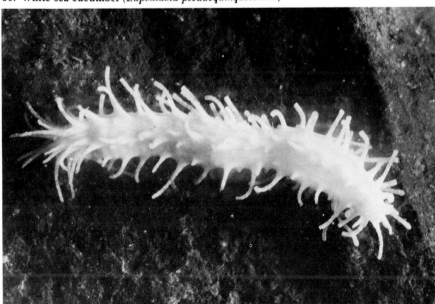

Rocky, *Protected*

Figure 61: This sea cucumber *(Psolus chitonoides)* confuses even marine biologists who are unfamiliar with it. It looks like a chiton because of its plates; however, there are three rows of tube feet on its underside, rather than the foot of a chiton. Its gills, when expanded (as in the photo), look like those of other sea cucumbers.

Figure 62: On a really rocky (rocks sitting on rocks, no sand) but protected beach, brittle or serpent stars may be found, although not too commonly. Several species of the genus *Ophiura* are possible in this photo. Though they have habits similar to their coastal relatives, they have thinner arms, smaller bodies, and are less brightly colored.

sea cucumber, starfish

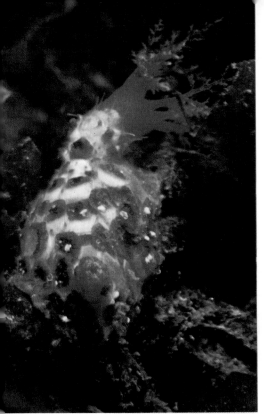

61. Chitonlike sea cucumber
(Psolus chitonoides)

62. Brittle or serpent star *(Ophiura)*

Rocky, *Protected*

Figure 63: Many kinds of crabs are numerous on protected rocky beaches. Most numerous is the purple shore crab *(Hemigrapsus nudus),* which occurs from the mid-tide region down almost to the lowest tide. Its most obvious feature is the purple color, which distinguishes it from the green shore crab *(Hemigrapsus oregonensis,* Figure 136). Some crabs of either species are mottled with white, leaving room for possible confusion about identity. This can be solved by looking for bristles on the tops of the walking legs — green shore crabs have them, while purple shore crabs are bare (hence the name *nudus*). Purple shore crabs prefer gravel and rock, while green shore crabs prefer at least a touch of mud. Thus, on a mud/gravel beach you can find both crabs living together. Both are important scavengers of dead animals and algae and contribute greatly to keeping beaches clean, the importance of the job being judged from the number of crabs present.

Figure 64: The hairy cancer crab *(Cancer oregonensis)* is not rare, but you are not likely to find more than a few in an hour of looking. Vaguely resembling the larger edible crabs, the shell is more nearly round, hairier, and lumpier than other *Cancer* crabs. Further, the maximum size is about one and one-half inches across the shell — never big enough to eat. It is found only in the low tide zone (compare to other *Cancer* crabs, Figures 103, 104, 105, and 137).

Figure 65: The black-clawed shore crab *(Lophopanopeus bellus)* has a distinctively angular shell and black-tipped claws. It lives under rocks that are exposed on only the lowest (minus) tides. It may be fairly abundant on some beaches such as Alki (Figure 46) or Blake Island (across from Alki), but is rare or absent on other beaches where it might also be expected, such as Sucia Island or along the shores of Camano Island State Park. The coloring is a drab mixture of purple and brown. When disturbed, this crab goes into a characteristic spread-eagle, stiff stance.

66

63. Purple shore crab *(Hemigrapsus nudus)*

64. Hairy cancer crab
(Cancer oregonensis)

65. Black-clawed shore crab *(Lophopanopeus bellus)*

Rocky, *Protected*

67. Kelp crab *(Pugettia producta)*

66. Decorator crab *(Oregonia gracilis)*

68. Sea anemone *(Tealia)*

Lynwood S. Smith

68

Figure 66: There are many species of decorator crabs found in tide pools and under rocks. They camouflage themselves with seaweed by gluing it on their backs and the tops of their legs, using a sticky saliva for glue. Often the seaweed continues to grow and eventually may completely hide the crab. Spider crabs in general, of which decorator crabs form a subgroup, are fairly inactive and largely unable to defend themselves (except the kelp crab, Figure 67), so being well disguised is important to their survival. *Oregonia gracilis* is pictured here; with slightly shorter legs, it could be *Scyra acutifrons,* although *Scyra* is not usually as vigorously decorated as *Oregonia.*

Figure 67: The kelp crab *(Pugettia producta)* is also a spider crab, but any seaweed on it just happened to grow there since the shell was last molted. This crab has extremely sharp points on its walking legs, allowing it to climb up the slippery stalks of brown kelps. It also may be found on piling and floats. In contrast to *Cancer* crabs (Figures 64, 103, 104, 105, 137), which cannot reach with their claws to the top of their shell, the kelp crab is difficult to handle because its claws reach to almost every point on its body — and rather quickly when compared with decorator crabs. Two points projecting forward from its shell above the "elbow" joint of its claws distinguish it from the decorator crab, which most often has a pear-shaped body. The patches of lighter color on the rock under the crab are coralline algae — a type of calcified alga — which feel like plaster or concrete to the touch (see also Figure 5 to see a clearer example of its purple color).

Figure 68: There is one large anemone found occasionally in the low tide zone on such solid rocky places as rock jetties or fill. It seems to have no common name except its generic name, *Tealia.* The tentacles have pale bands of color, sometimes with a drab greenish background color. The body is either entirely red or streaked with red, depending on the species. This anemone can grow rather large, up to four inches high and six inches across when expanded.

Rocky, *Protected*

Figure 69: Nudibranchs are to the seashore what butterflies are to the land — colorful, a bit hard to find, delicate, and prized by collectors. Nudibranchs, related to snails, must either taste bad or have some other subtle defense (see Figure 145, the opalescent nudibranch) because they have no shells, rarely hide or camouflage themselves, and yet seem not to be attacked by any of the common predators. One large category of nudibranchs, of which the sea lemon (*Archidoris montereyensis,* pictured here) is an example, are called dorids (see also Figures 32, 33, 71). They are characterized by a ruffly frill of gills surrounding the anus and, in the case of the sea lemon, by a skin which has the appearance of an old lemon peeling. The exact shade and color of skin varies from a dirty orange to white, sometimes also having small black spots, depending on which species of *Archidoris* or the similar-appearing *Anisodoris* or *Acanthodoris* you have in hand. The most common species on gravel and rocky beaches is *Archidoris montereyensis.* Most species eat sponge; a few eat bryozoans (moss animals, similar to hydroids, Figure 140).

Figure 70: A somewhat less common but more spectacular sea lemon is pure white with a bright lemon yellow edging *(Cadlina luteomarginata).* It also eats sponges.

Figure 71: One of the most spectacular dorid nudibranchs, *Triopha carpenteri,* is almost unbelievably gaudy — white with fluorescent orange trimming. It can be several inches long, although the larger specimens are usually sub-tidal. It eats bryozoans.

70

69. Sea lemon *(Archidoris montereyensis)*

71. Dorid nudibranch *(Triopha carpenteri)*

70. Sea lemon *(Cadlina luteomarginata)*

Rocky, *Protected*

Figure 72: Another group of nudibranchs, the dendronotids, are characterized by branched, rather than single, projections from the upper side of the body. The typical coloring is white with purple tips on the projections, although there are many color variations. The intertidal species are two to three inches long, but larger subtidal species may be eight to twelve inches long (various species of *Dendronotus*). Most eat the sea anemone-like stages of jellyfish and can be found on floats as well as on rocks. I have seen large specimens swim by folding the edges of the foot together lengthwise and then flexing the body rapidly from side to side.

Nudibranch eggs are laid in characteristic delicate ribbons, and usually are the same color as the nudibranch. The ribbon disintegrates as the eggs develop into free-swimming larval stages and swim away (see Figure 50).

Figure 73: Scallops are most common subtidally but occasionally show up in the lower intertidal zone. They are unusual bivalves in several ways. Seen here in an aquarium, they mostly just hang by a unique stalklike foot with a suction cup on the end. Though they appear to do nothing, they are actually filtering food from large volumes of water, which they pump (with cilia) through their gills. If you look closely around the edge of the mantle near the shell's edge, you will see regularly spaced, gold-colored beads. These are eyespots which detect shadows and movement of large objects nearby, though they do not see images in the same sense that we do. Also, most scallops can swim to escape predators (usually starfish) by clapping their shells together rapidly, producing jets of water on each side of the hinge, and giving the ridiculous appearance of a pair of false teeth eating their way through the water. The two shells are not quite symmetrical, the shell on the bottom usually being a little more deeply curved than the top shell. Also, the top shell often has a special sponge (found nowhere else) growing on it, while the bottom shell is clean. A scallop this small is not worth taking for eating unless you eat all of it — which is quite acceptable, although usually just the muscle is consumed. (This photo could be any of several species of *Pecten* — species differences are based on minor shell variations.)

72. **Dendronotid nudibranch** *(Dendronotus)*

73. **Scallop** *(Pecten)*

Rocky, *Protected*

Figure 74: The rock scallop *(Hinnites giganteus)* looks and acts much like its free-swimming cousins for about a year after hatching, but then cements its lower shell solidly to a rock and is fixed for the rest of its life. The shells become very thick, heavy, and encrusted with many kinds of plants and animals, making them difficult to find once they close their shells and cover their bright orange mantle (the flesh next to the shell). A bright yellow sponge may also be found embedded in the thick shell, appearing on the surface as small yellow patches. Most rock scallops are now found subtidally because all of the intertidal ones have been taken for food except on the most remote beaches. The muscle in rock scallops is particularly large and delicious. Check your local sport catch regulations for scallops; there is usually a catch limit and sometimes a size limit, depending on the area.

75. Piddock *(Pholadidea)*

Figure 75: Piddocks are also highly specialized bivalves but are very different from scallops. The piddock bores in hard clay and soft rock by mechanically rotating its shell against the bottom of the hole. As the piddock grows, it also burrows deeper, creating a tapered hole from which it has no way out. The foot of a piddock sucks onto the bottom of the hole and special muscles rotate and rock the shell against the rock walls of the hole. These muscles are attached to projections inside the shells which curve out from the hinge area. The hinge is especially broad and flexible to allow this action. The siphon (neck) also has rough scales on its surface to scour the sides of the hole above the shell as the siphon increases its diameter. The smaller piddocks *(Pholadidea,* illustrated) bore in solid rock while the larger ones *(Zirfaea,* not shown) bore in clay and can be mistaken for gweducs. The siphons of piddocks are divided — compare with the gweduc siphon in Figure 107.

74

76. Purple sea urchin
(Strongylocentrotus droebachiensis)

74. Rock scallop *(Hinnites giganteus)*

Figure 76: While the sea urchin of the coast (Figure 41) is purple, the sea urchin of protected waters is smaller (rarely over four inches across) and green. In most other respects it is like its coastal cousin — inhabits the low tide zone, is sometimes under rocks (but doesn't bore holes in the rock), eats algae, and has edible eggs. Its scientific name, *Strongylocentrotus droebachiensis,* is one of the longest there is. A third species of urchin (*S. franciscanus,* Figure 7), usually called the red urchin, is less common and usually subtidal. It is purple, red, or orange and has much longer spines than either the purple or green urchin. I have seen it most often on a few solid rock faces in the San Juan Islands, although it occurs subtidally all along our coast.

Rocky, *Protected*

Figure 77: Seeing fish out of water at low tide is surprising to some people, but these survive quite well as long as they can stay moist and cool. There are four major groups of intertidal fish — clingfish (Figures 43, 44), cottids, also called sculpins or bullheads (Figure 94), pricklebacks, and gunnels. The last two collectively are called blennies or blenny eels although they are not true eels. The fish here *(Anoplarchus purpurescens)* is specifically called the cockscomb prickleback, but the older name of crested blenny is also used. Both names refer to the fleshy crest on top of its head which runs down to its snout. The black and white coloring is typical, although somewhat changeable, depending on the background colors. Two other fish, the saddleback gunnel and the penpoint gunnel (Figure 123), are common along with the cockscomb prickleback. They have more varied coloration, lack the fleshy crest, but are about the same size.

Protected rocky beaches can have a great variety of large seaweeds, which can usually be classified as red, green, or brown. Identifying these is a special study of its own, especially with the red seaweeds, many of which are not red but vary from purplish brown through shades of red to a steel gray. Some are commercially important as sources of algin and carrageenin, both used as thickeners and emulsifying agents in foods.

Figure 78: There are three species of octopus in Puget Sound. The specimen shown intertidally (at Clallam Bay) is probably *Octopus leioderma,* one of the two smaller species. The other small species is unnamed and more common subtidally. Both species rarely exceed a couple of pounds and have slimmer, longer arms in proportion to their body size than the largest of the three species, *Octopus dofleini,* which can exceed 100 pounds. This is the octopus taken by divers and exhibited in public aquariums. The large octopus captures and eats a variety of food, including crabs, scallops, and small fishes. In turn, octopuses are hunted by lingcod and man. The small species may reside intertidally on transitional and protected rocky beaches, but the large species is seen there only occasionally. The octopus is the smartest of the invertebrate animals. It has elaborate behavior, including rapid color changes, and can, with patience, be taught simple tricks.

76

77. Cockscomb prickleback *(Anoplarchus purpurescens)*

78. Octopus

5

Gravel beaches

Exposed and Transitional Gravel Beaches – Examples

Figure 79: Clallam Bay and Agate Beach, west of Port Angeles, Washington, are fairly exposed (transitional) gravel beaches. Biologically these beaches are deserts — the constant tumbling of the gravel by surf lets nothing survive for long. Gravel forms by the breaking up of rocky headlands through freezing and wave action. The rocky headlands at the ends of the beaches are typical rocky habitat once you get far enough away from damage by wave-flung gravel. (Note: At the time of this writing, Agate Beach was private, but open to the public for an admission fee.)

There are a number of other transitional gravel beaches on the Strait of Juan de Fuca and in the San Juan Islands. Much of the south side of San Juan

79. Transitional gravel beach, Clallam Bay, Wa.

79

Gravel, *Exposed*/Gravel, *Protected*

Island, facing the Strait of Juan de Fuca, consists of exposed gravel beach with occasional rocky headlands. The end result — the dearth of life — is the same, but the origin of the gravel is different. Here sand and gravel bluffs slowly erode onto the beach. The sand gets carried away quickly, leaving almost pure gravel. The subtidal features of transitional gravel beaches may differ widely. While Agate Beach is very steep with deep water close to shore, on the south shore of Sucia Island in the San Juans a large sand flat extends from the gravel beach subtidally.

The northern beach of Deception Pass State Park on Whidbey Island, Washington, is near the place where the tide reaches its greatest velocity. Without the fast-running tide and the turbulence it produces, this gravel beach might be somewhat protected and productive. However, the beach is sterile, like those above, due to gravel movement.

Jones Island State Park in the central San Juan Islands has two gravel beaches that face the winter storms. The beaches are just barely stable enough for marine animals, their presence indicated by a dark band of kelp usually seen along the low tide line of each beach. Expect very limited fauna here.

Protected Gravel Beaches – Examples and Species

Turn Island State Park (undeveloped) near Friday Harbor, Washington, demonstrates several kinds of beaches and degrees of exposure. The outer bays, facing south, are almost rocky and have limited fauna. The little bay on the west is more protected and has a gravelly sand bottom with some eelgrass growing there. The beach to the north is intermediate in type between the two other beaches. Thus three quite different habitats occur only a few hundred feet apart. At both Jones and Turn islands the rocky points at the ends of the beaches play important roles in preventing the substrate material of the beach from being washed away.

Sequim Bay State Park is typical of many Puget Sound beaches where there is no massive bluff above the beach. The beach is fairly flat, trees come down to the high tide line, and a small stream delivers a steady supply of sand and gravel — in this case somewhat faster than it is being removed, since a small delta is forming.

Camp Casey on Whidbey Island once guarded the entrance to Puget Sound but is now a state park with a variety of beaches. The substrate is basically sand and gravel, as is most of Whidbey Island. The outer beaches are comparatively exposed and barren, the bay is more sheltered and productive, and the breakwater is typical rock habitat.

Lincoln Park in West Seattle is another example of the wide range of combinations of substrate and exposure. At the western end of the park, the rounded point is mostly sterile, movable gravel. Farther back in the bay, the

80

beach is more protected. Here, there are some larger rocks, so the beach approaches being a protected rocky beach. At the back of the bay, the substrate is muddy sand.

Golden Gardens Park, just outside Seattle's ship canal, is similar to Lincoln Park except that the beach faces north instead of south. Its westernmost point is sterile gravel, but because winter storms come from the south, the point largely protects the sandy beach at the north end of the park. Only a small amount of rock (which came from the railroad fill) remains above the sand there. The marina breakwaters to the south also provide extensive habitat for protected rocky shore animals and plants.

Camano Head, at the southern end of Camano Island, represents a typical Puget Sound shoreline — eroding bluffs above a sand and gravel beach. Although privately owned (beach access from the land is difficult), boaters have dug clams here for many years. The beach at Camano Head is a typical mixture of bare cobble and gravel (on the upper part of the beach) with sand flats lower on the beach.

Figure 80: Kopachuck State Park is similar to Camano Head, except that the gravel bluffs above the beach are not as high, and the sand is a little more prominent. The clam digger's usual strategy is to work as far down on the beach as possible to reach areas that are exposed least often. This may leave good clamming areas undug higher on the beach during a really low tide. Most clam diggers believe that wave action will fill their holes. The fallacy of this is well illustrated by the mounds and holes you can see on many clam beaches — left by diggers from days and weeks earlier.

80. Protected gravel beach, Kopachuck State Park, Wa.

81

Gravel, *Protected*

Figure 81: Three species of clams are common throughout Puget Sound's gravel beaches — (left to right) the butter or Washington clam, the native littleneck clam, and the bent-nose clam. The butter clam *(Saxidomus giganteus)* has only concentric lines on its shell and is almost always white. It can grow to a shell length of five inches or more in six to eight years, but rarely attains that length on a heavily dug beach. Small butter clams are steamed and eaten whole like littlenecks, usually dipped in melted butter, while larger ones are opened by hand and ground up for chowder. Butter clams may bury themselves up to a foot deep. The native littleneck *(Venerupis staminea;* an older name still heard sometimes is *Protothaca staminea)* is also found along the low tide line up to six inches deep but contains much more meat. Littlenecks are also called steamer clams because they never grow more than about two inches in length — too small to open by hand. The outside of the shell is basically white, although sometimes stained by beach coloration; it has both radial and concentric lines. The bent-nose clam *(Macoma nasuta)* is small, thin, and is so named because the narrow end of its shell bends to one side. It prefers sandy/mud beaches and is quite edible, although it usually contains sand unless left to clean itself in clean seawater at least overnight. Bent-nose clams are rarely more than two to four inches below the surface. (Its "unbent" relative, *Macoma inquinata,* is also common, Figure 82).

81. Left to right: butter clam *(Saxidomus giganteus),* native littleneck clam *(Venerupis staminea),* bent-nose clam *(Macoma nasuta)*

The gravel/mud beach in front of the Washington State Shellfish Lab at Whitney Point (Dabob Bay, off Hood Canal, south of the town of Quilcene) is well protected. Clam digging at the water's edge produces native littlenecks, and near the middle of the beach, Japanese littleneck or Manila clams (Figure 82). These clams are barely under the gravel — usually the top of the shell is only one inch below the surface — and can be dug without a shovel. They were accidentally imported into Washington with Japanese oyster seed many years ago, and have adapted to a niche not otherwise occupied on our beaches. They are now as popular a steamer clam as the native littleneck.

Figure 82: The Manila (also called Japanese) littleneck *(Venerupis japonica, also called Tapes philippinarium),* seen on the left in the photo, has a somewhat more elongated shell than the native littleneck. It is rarely white; colors may be various mixtures of brown, olive-drab, purple, and green and may appear in stripes, in sunbursts radiating from the hinge, or the predominant form — irregular blotches. Inside the shell, there is almost always some purple coloring next to the siphon (neck). The internal anatomy and flavor is essentially the same as the native littleneck.

The clams shown in the photograph, dug at Kopachuck State Park, include the butter clam (center) and a macoma *(Macoma inquinata,* on the right), which resembles the bent-nose clam (Figure 81) except that the shell does not bend to one side.

82. Left to right: Manila littleneck clam *(Venerupis japonica),* **butter clam** *(Saxidomus giganteus),* **macoma clam** *(Macoma inquinata)*

Gravel, *Protected*

Figure 83: The moon snail *(Polinices lewisii)* is part of the fauna of most clam beaches but is not often seen because it spends most of its time burrowing below the surface where it feeds on clams. It does this by rasping a hole through the side of the clam's shell with its radula (similar to that in chitons, Figure 38). Its large foot is filled mostly with water and can be drawn entirely inside the shell by squirting out large volumes of water when the need for protection arises.

83. Moon snail *(Polinices lewisii)*

84. Sand collar — eggs of the moon snail

Figure 84: Almost anyone who has been on clam beaches in spring has seen sand collars, but few realize that they are the eggs of the moon snail. The snail extrudes the collar between two folds of its foot and constructs it from sand, eggs (which are about the size of sand grains), and mucus. As the eggs hatch and leave for the free-swimming part of their life cycle, the sand collar disintegrates.

Gravel, *Protected*

Figure 85: Clam diggers may occasionally dig up a marine crayfish, also called a mud shrimp *(Upogebia pugettensis)*. It makes burrows in firm, preferably muddy gravel and lines them smoothly with fine sand or mud. The burrows may be two feet deep (deeper than most clam diggers go) and usually have two openings. The shrimp digs, using its flattened claws as scoops, and then fans water through the burrow with its abdominal appendages (swimmerets) to filter out food particles. Its grayish color, hairiness, and generally more substantial body distinguish it from the ghost shrimp found under similar circumstances on sandy beaches (Figure 109).

86. Scale worm *(Halosydna brevisetosa)*

Figure 86: Scale worms are a group of segmented worms having a row of overlapping scales on each side of their bodies. On gravel beaches, they are most easily found on the undersides of mottled starfishes (Figure 50), although not every starfish will have one. The scale worm benefits by helping itself to whatever the starfish eats, but may or may not help the starfish in return for the free food. Each species of symbiotic scale worm selects only certain species of starfish. Those species of scale worms that are free-living (nonsymbiotic) are not normally hitchhikers. They are found under rocks but are not numerous. The specimen illustrated is *Halosydna brevisetosa.*

Figure 87: The pile worm *(Nereis vexillosa)* is also often seen on gravel beaches. It burrows into the mussels layered on rocks and piling and is also found under rocks that rest on gravel. When there are no rocks, the worm may burrow shallowly in the gravel itself. Its color is normally a slightly iridescent green. During warm summer evenings the pile worm leaves its burrow to swim in large swarms, at which time it reproduces by releasing eggs and sperm into the water. This species rarely grows more than twelve inches in length, but a related species *(N. brandti)* may attain nearly three feet and measure as big around as your finger. Both species are equipped with a pair of curved black pincers inside an eversible snout, which are used to tear off the seaweed they eat.

86

85. Marine crayfish or mud shrimp *(Upogebia pugettensis)*

87. Pile worm *(Nereis vexillosa)*

Gravel, *Protected*

88. Peanut worms *(Phascolosoma agassizii)*

89. Hairy hermit crab
(Pagurus hirsutiusculus) in whelk shell

90. Hermit crab *(Pagurus ochotensis)*

88

worm, hermit crab

Figure 88: Peanut worms *(Phascolosoma agassizii)* are nonsegmented worms found under rocks in gravel or in gravel-filled crevices in solid rock. They are so named because they approximate the size and hardness of an unshelled peanut. They are also called sipunculid worms, after the name of their small phylum in zoological classification.

Figure 89: For some reason, hermit crabs are considered clownish. Perhaps carrying around a snail shell (here a well-worn whelk shell) to protect a soft abdomen, and to hide in if the shell is large enough, gives the hermit crab a clownish awkwardness. When snail shells are scarce, hermit crabs appear equally ridiculous carrying a shell that is too small. The hairy hermit crab *(Pagurus hirsutiusculus)* is the most common on gravel beaches and is generally drab in color except for the white bands on its legs. Young hairy hermit crabs may use periwinkle or other smaller snail shells. Some people have wondered whether hermit crabs kill snails to get their shells, but there is no evidence of this; hermit crabs in general are scavengers. A related hermit crab *(P. granosimanus)* is of similar size and coloring. In contrast, this crab is hairless, lacks the colored bands, and lives lower on the beach.

Figure 90: The larger, more colorful hermit crabs are usually subtidal. This specimen *(Pagurus ochotensis)* is large enough to use a moon snail shell (Figure 83). Other large hermit crabs may use the shell of the hairy triton *(Fusitriton oregonensis),* which is also most common subtidally. Being spectacular, larger hermit crabs are often featured in public aquarium displays where it is possible to get a close look at the remarkable variety of head and mouth appendages these animals have. Their eyestalks and antennae usually stand erect. Other leglike structures serve to hold, sort, and grind food. When all of this equipment is in action, one has the feeling that the hermit crab was designed by Walt Disney as an impossibly complex hay baler.

89

Gravel, *Protected*

Figure 91: Coon-stripe shrimp *(Pandalus danae)* occur intertidally when immature but migrate into deeper water as they grow larger. They may also occur on deeper piling or hang under floats. As adults they are an important food species, along with several other shrimp which are always subtidal, and are caught in pots or trawls. Irregular diagonal stripes are characteristic of the coon-stripe shrimp.

Crustaceans in general and shrimp in particular are beautiful to look at under low-power magnification. Then you can see that their color is composed of tiny dots of many colors. By controlling the size of each dot, the shrimp can change color to approximate that of its background.

Figure 92: While the coon-stripe shrimp described in the previous figure is sought for its meat, the broken-back shrimp, the most common shrimp in protected rocky or gravelly tide pools, is much smaller and perhaps goes unnoticed. When you first approach a tide pool or a pool under a rock, there is a great scramble among the animals to find a hiding place. Unless you watch carefully for these half-inch to inch-long shrimp, they will have disappeared by means of their excellent camouflage capabilities. A variety of colors are possible — browns, greens, whites, some blue — in solid colors, speckles, patches, or large patterns. Because of their changeability, identification must be made by various structural features — legs, mouthparts, spines, etc. Two of the more common genera are *Hippolyte* and *Spirontocaris,* but it is easier simply to refer to all of them as broken-back shrimp, as long as they have the humped tail (abdomen) like the one in the picture.

shrimp

91. **Coon-stripe shrimp** *(Pandalus danae)*

92. **Broken-back shrimp**

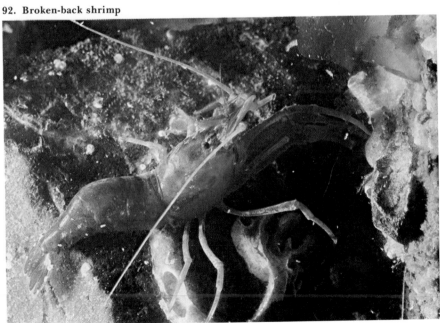

Gravel, *Protected*

Figure 93: The California sea cucumber *(Parastichopus californicus)* is found in tide pools and subtidally, where it feeds on the fine organic debris that settles out in calm waters. Its mouth appendages resemble tiny mops, and the cucumber licks them clean as they accumulate debris. Cucumbers must taste bad to most predators because their brownish red color and pseudospines (they are actually soft and fleshy) are hardly inconspicuous. Up to eighteen inches long, they do not easily hide, yet I have never seen any other animals eating them.

When relaxed, the cucumber looks like a large flexible bag full of water, but when the muscles in the body wall tighten up, its shape can become quite rigid. Perhaps because of excessive internal pressure and sometimes under conditions of high water temperature and low oxygen (commonly in the specimen collector's bucket), the cucumber may rupture at one end and spew out its delicate internal organs. This does not kill the animal because the internal organs, mostly a thin-walled digestive tract, are readily replaced, but it is still questionable whether this has any survival value. The long white strips of muscle on the inside of the body wall are edible.

Figure 94: The tide pool sculpin occurs in a wide range of habitats from rather exposed to quite protected. This picture shows a greenish sculpin in a tide pool. These fish cannot be identified by color pattern. Given twenty minutes to change, they can turn into almost any combination of black and white, reddish brown, green, blue green, or a solid color version of any one of those. The only stable color seems to be the white spot at the base of the caudal (tail) fin. Technical identification is performed by counting fin rays, the number and shape of spines on the gill covers, etc. However, there are only two species of *Oligocottus,* and the most common one by far is *Oligocottus maculosus,* so your chance of guessing the correct species name is good without all this fuss. The maximum size is about one and one-half inches long.

Figure 95: An illustration of the tide pool sculpin's ability to change color, this is the same species as seen in Figure 94, placed on a different background. It can also change to blue green, gray, brown, as well as the green and black color phases that have been illustrated. Usually, only the white spot at the base of the tail remains unchanged, although the white patch behind the dorsal fin is usually visible.

92

sea cucumber, fish

93. California sea cucumber
   (Parastichopus californicus)

94. Tide pool sculpin
   (Oligocottus maculosus)

95. Tide pool sculpin, color variation

6

Sandy beaches

Exposed and Transitional Sandy Beaches – Examples and Species

Figure 96: There are many miles of surf-beaten sandy shores found along the coasts of Oregon, Washington, and British Columbia. This photo is a view northward from Cape Blanco, Oregon. When scalloping of the shoreline by the surf is evident, sand is being moved seaward in the low spots and shoreward on the high spots. These circulation cells are caused by water moving laterally along the beach as well as back and forth with each wave. Animals living in such an area must be prepared to dig rapidly upward or downward to keep from being washed out or buried by such movable sand.

In Washington, when the tide is out, the upper half of the damp sand is designated a roadway, but driving on the razor clam beds on the lower half of the beach is prohibited. The successful driver stays below the sand that is dry enough to be unstable and above the shiny sand, which has enough water in it to also be unstable.

96. Exposed sandy beach, Cape Blanco, Or.

Sandy, *Exposed*

Figure 97: The dominant species of the coastal sandy beach is the razor clam *(Siliqua patula)*. While shell lengths of over eight inches occur in clams on remote beaches, the typical size on well-dug beaches ranges from two to four inches. Razor clams feed on the brown scum and other suspended matter that wash back and forth on the sand, so they must stay close to the surface. When feeding, the siphon may stretch upward an inch or more beyond the shell, and if the foot is stretched downward an equal distance, then the clam's first digging effort will move the top of the siphon two inches downward. It typically moves down another inch every second or so with each successive extension and retraction of the foot. An undamaged clam put in a pool of water will usually demonstrate its digging abilities.

Capturing razor clams usually requires fast digging, and there are several strategies for finding them. Experienced diggers walk in the water and watch for the exposed tip of a clam siphon to make a slight "V" in the receding wave and then dig after it with one or two quick shovelfuls before the next wave. Other diggers walk backward or tap the moist sand with their shovels and watch for a dry spot to form suddenly, showing that a clam was stimulated into digging downward there. Given this kind of a running start, the clam usually can dig down twelve to eighteen inches before you can catch up with it, and a wave often fills the hole before you find the clam. Other diggers work above the wave zone and dig at any little dimple in the sand that looks like a clam had dug down there some time ago. This means moving more sand than by the other methods, but usually gets you a clam if you dig deeply enough. Be sure to check local regulations before digging.

Many razor clams are damaged, especially when dug by inexperienced persons, so that diggers in Washington are required to keep every clam they capture. Most clams dug up and then returned to the beach die shortly afterward — they are fragile animals in spite of their rugged environment. Thus, putting back small razor clams is wasteful.

Figure 98: There are relatively few animals besides razor clams that can survive on exposed sandy beaches. One of those is a spectacularly large sand hopper *(Orchestoidea californiana)* which burrows in the dry sand at the high tide line, often under or near kelp or eelgrass that has come ashore. The sand hoppers may be over an inch long, including antennae. They come out mainly at night; however, you can find them by digging wherever there are clusters of holes in the sand. You may also find smaller gray sand hoppers in the same location. Other sandy-beach inhabitants include a mole crab, one small sea louse, and a small shrimp, all of which burrow rapidly, are well camouflaged, and difficult to find. You may see empty shells of Dungeness crabs (Figure 103) on the beach because the crabs live just beyond the surf.

96

97. Razor clam *(Siliqua patula)*

98. Sand hopper *(Orchestoidea californiana)*

Sandy, *Exposed*

99. Exposed sandy beach near La Push, Wa.

Figure 99: Traveling north from Grays Harbor, Washington, the supply of sand (mostly from the Columbia River) decreases, and the beaches become increasingly rocky. Razor clams seem fairly scarce on rockier beaches, even though their distribution extends as far north as Alaska, wherever there are adequately exposed sandy beaches. This photo shows a portion of beach near La Push. Most of the sand may have come from the Soleduck River, as well as other rivers to the south and the small creek in the foreground.

Figure 100: Crescent Beach, west of Port Angeles, faces the Strait of Juan de Fuca but is protected from the effects of the westerly ground swell by a rocky headland in the background. The beach is transitional between coastal and protected types — too exposed for most protected-type fauna, but too protected for razor clams, etc. Some seaweed growth is visible from a boat as dark patches below the low tide line. (Note: This beach is privately owned but has been open to the public by admission fee.)

Dungeness Spit, on the south shore of the Strait of Juan de Fuca, illustrates how sand is transported along a shoreline. The headland to the west causes currents along the shore to swerve outward and drop any sand being carried. The spit thus follows the edge of the fast current and turns parallel to the shore when influenced by other currents farther offshore. The spit is still growing — when the lighthouse was built many years ago, it was located at

100. Transitional sandy beach, Crescent Beach, west of Port Angeles, Wa.

the tip of the spit. Now the spit extends half a mile beyond the lighthouse. Dungeness Spit is the namesake home of the Dungeness crab (Figure 103), which was once abundant in the vicinity, especially in the extensive eelgrass beds in the bay inside the spit. Long-time residents there say that before World War I, any crab less than ten inches across the back of the shell was thrown back. Most residents of the Pacific Northwest less than fifty years old have never caught a crab that large. Outside a protected area like this bay, Dungeness crabs would be found only subtidally in the Strait of Juan de Fuca.

There are several transitional sandy beaches along the shores of the eastern end of the Strait of Juan de Fuca. Fort Flagler, now a state park, used to guard the entrance to Puget Sound near Port Townsend. It faces Whidbey Island, which also has mostly sandy beaches facing the Strait, such as the beach at Camp Casey.

Bowman Bay is just north of Deception Pass and faces the westerly ground swell from the Stait of Juan de Fuca. As above, this transitional sandy beach has little fauna, while the rocky sides of the bay are moderately productive. At the time of publication the facilities here included some concrete ponds with pumped seawater and a few fish, under control of the U.S. Fish and Wildlife Service and generally open to the public.

Sandy, *Protected*

Protected Sandy Beaches – Examples and Species

There are many sandy beaches in Puget Sound. Many in southern Puget Sound are sandy because the waterways are narrow enough to drastically limit the size of waves that can occur there, and the tidal currents are also insufficient to carry sand away. This includes part of the beach at Kopachuck State Park, west of Tacoma, which appears to have considerable movement of sand northward along the beach. However, there is also some eelgrass near low water, indicating fairly stable areas which might produce clams and other fauna.

At Twanoh State Park in southern Hood Canal there is gravel in the creek outflow and sand elsewhere, with some tendency for the sand to be muddy at the lowest tide levels.

The tidal flats at the mouth of the Dosewallips River on the west shore of central Hood Canal are partly private and partly public. They are considered some of the better beaches for digging gweduc clams (Figures 106, 107) and wading for Dungeness crabs (Figure 103). This extensive area varies from pea gravel to muddy sand.

Figure 101: Typical sandy beaches of Puget Sound are often composed of gravel at the high tide line and sand farther down. Gravelly bluffs just behind the beach supply the sand and gravel. Wave action, especially during winter storms, sorts the sand and gravel according to size. This photo is of Alki Beach, with downtown Seattle in the background. While rockier than some beaches and lacking the gravel bluff behind the beach, this portion of Alki still falls within the general category of typical sand and gravel beaches.

101. Protected sand and gravel beach, portion of Alki Beach, Seattle, Wa.

Sandy, *Protected*

Figure 102: An estuary is a region where fresh water mixes with salt water. Usually estuaries occur at the mouth of a river or creek, but there are often freshwater seepages at the foot of gravel bluffs bordering beaches where ground water surfaces. Having to adjust to a freshwater habitat at low tide and a saltwater habitat at high tide is a challenge few organisms can master, even though many prefer a steady dilution of salt water (oysters, for example). One seaweed that thrives in this alternating environment is a green seaweed, *Enteromorpha intestinalis.* It has the same color as sea lettuce, but is tubular and wrinkled in texture. As shown here, it needs a rock to attach to, but otherwise seems to tolerate being surrounded by sand.

Figure 103: The Dungeness crab *(Cancer magister)* is a major species sought along the shores of sandy beaches, often by wading out below the low tide line on shallow sand flats and in eelgrass beds. Its tannish purple color is characteristic, as is the shape of its shell, especially the shape of the teeth along the front edge of the shell. These crabs may burrow backwards into the sand to hide during low tide, with just the eyes and mouth exposed, or they may be mobile and travel as much as a mile a day. Dungeness crabs are scavengers of dead fish, clams, and other fauna. They are popular sport species, so check local regulations.

Figure 104: The red crab or rock crab *(Cancer productus)* is often found with the Dungeness crab but will also inhabit rockier areas where the Dungeness crab is not found. In contrast to the Dungeness, the body and legs of the rock crab are smaller, and the claws larger. Its dark red color is typical, and most specimens have black-tipped claws. The red crab preys on clams and oysters, using its powerful claws to crush the shells and tear the meat into edible-sized pieces. Since it is a predator of valued species, there is no size or catch limit for red crabs in Washington, but be sure of your identification before taking rock crabs in any other than the ways prescribed for Dungeness crabs.

102. Green seaweed
(Enteromorpha intestinalis)
in estuary region

104. Red or rock crab
(Cancer productus)

103. Dungeness crab *(Cancer magister)*

Lynwood S. Smith

Sandy, *Protected*

Figure 105: Immature rock crabs are found under rocks on rocky/gravel beaches more often than the adults. The odd purplish or brownish tint of their ornate striping is highly distinctive. Except for their shell shape, they do not resemble the adult rock crab.

106. Gweduc clam *(Panope generosa)*

Figure 106: The gweduc clam (also geoduck, pronounced gooeyduck, *Panope generosa*) is the largest bivalve in Puget Sound, with record specimens exceeding fifteen pounds live weight. However, the average clam digger is more likely to find them in the three- to six-pound range and feel lucky at that. Their huge siphons can extend as much as three or four feet to reach the surface, where they filter food from the water. Anyone who has obtained his daily limit of gweducs (presently three per digger) has done a hard day's work.

Figure 107: This is a gweduc siphon (neck) seen in gravel. There are only two other siphons nearly this large — those of the black horse clam (Figure 108) and the clay-boring piddock (Figure 75, siphon not shown), which is split into separate tubes for the last three to four inches. Be a little wary of looking down the holes in the siphon — a large gweduc can squirt a one-inch-diameter stream of water for several feet when it starts to pull its siphon down.

There are extensive subtidal gweduc beds, which are being commercially harvested by scuba divers and marketed under the trade name "King Clam" to seafood and gourmet restaurants.

104

105. Immature rock crab

107. Gweduc siphon or neck

Sandy, *Protected*

108. Horse clam (*Tresus nuttallii*)

Figure 108: Horse clams (*Tresus nuttallii* or *T. capax*, both very similar) are the second largest clams in Puget Sound. Their desirability is a matter of personal preference. According to some, the meat is tough and strong-flavored; others say that, since the flavor of ordinary clams is lost in chowder, horse clams are just right. They are fairly adaptable, living in everything from gravelly to muddy sand, although their classic habitat is probably open sand, as at Cultus or Useless bays at the southern end of Whidbey Island. Burrowing depth is a maximum of about two feet, as little as one foot in relatively firm sand. This bivalve is also called gaper clam, horse neck clam, or rubber neck clam.

Figure 109: A number of animals are uncovered while digging for clams. One common inhabitant of soft sand is the ghost shrimp (*Callianassa californiensis*) whose burrows are marked by a small mound of "tailings." This ghostly pale orange shrimp is delicate in structure and coloring and frequently damaged by being dug up. In soft sand it can soon disappear again, however, with or without a burrow. It feeds on organic matter sorted out from the sand and mud in which it burrows.

Figure 110: A number of segmented worms (genus *Glycera*) will be found in soft sand. They make those small holes you wonder about when looking for places to dig clams. In large part they feed like earthworms, eating their way through the ground and digesting its organic matter. The glycerid (also called corrugated) worm is a rapid burrower, using a large pink proboscis with four black hooks on the end which it everts before it to capture prey. It also seems to use the proboscis as a ram for pushing into the sand.

109. Ghost shrimp *(Callianassa californiensis)*

110. Glycerid worm *(Glycera)*

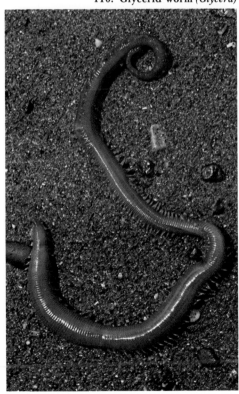

Sandy, *Protected*

Figure 111: Puget Sound's largest and most spectacular starfish is the sunflower star *(Pycnopodia helianthoides)*. The color and number of rays are variable. I have seen one specimen with forty-four rays that was over thirty-six inches in diameter! The rays are easily torn off and are apparently regenerated just as readily. The body is soft and flexible. The underside is a mass of tube feet with which the sunflower star can really run, at least by starfish standards. I timed one moving at ten feet per minute. Sunflower stars are wide-ranging predators of bivalves, sand dollars, and probably sea urchins. They will also scavenge. They range over rock, gravel, and sand bottoms subtidally, perhaps even digging up clams (I have seen them in washbasin-sized depressions eating clams). Many animals respond to their presence — scallops swim; cockles extend their feet violently and repeatedly to hop away as though on pogo sticks; giant cucumbers practically gallop to get out of their way; and sand dollars rapidly burrow beneath the sand.

Figure 112: The uncommon rose star *(Crossaster papposus)* is beautifully distinctive with concentric color rings and usually ten rays. It is probably a predator like most other starfish.

111. **Sunflower starfish** *(Pycnopodia helianthoides)*

112. **Rose starfish** *(Crossaster papposus)*

113. Sun starfish *(Solaster stimpsoni)*

114. Frosted nudibranch *(Dirona albolineata)*

Figure 113: Another starfish with more than five rays, which might be confused with either of the two previous starfish, is the sun starfish *(Solaster stimpsoni)*. The radiating color bands are characteristic, although the colors on some specimens are weaker than shown in the picture. It is found both intertidally and subtidally and is about as uncommon as *Crossaster*, although not necessarily found in the same areas.

Figure 114: The large frosted nudibranch *(Dirona albolineata)* eats snails as well as some tunicates and moss animals (bryozoans). The plumes on its back are extensions of its body wall rather than gills. Although I have spotted this nudibranch most often while snorkeling over sandy bottoms, its food suggests that it is also found on rocks and floats. A related species *(Dirona aurantia)* is an orange sherbet color with white tips and edges on the plumes.

Figure 115: Few snails are at home on sand, tending to be more suited to solid footing on rocks, floats, etc. However, these snails with distinctively attractive shells occur in large numbers on the Dosewallips tideflats of the Olympic Peninsula. They have no common name that I know of, although a similarly shaped group of species under the genus *Bittium* are called screw shells. Pictured is *Batillaria zonalis;* it likes sandy, even fairly muddy beaches and was introduced from Japan with oyster seed. Thus, it is most common in areas where Pacific oyster seed from Japan has been planted, such as Hood Canal.

115. Snails *(Batillaria zonalis)*

Lynwood S. Smith

111

Sandy, *Protected*

Figure 116: Although sand dollars *(Dendraster excentricus)* occur on many beaches where the sand is soft, few people see them because they are usually buried during low tide. When feeding, they stand nearly vertically, about half-exposed. Microscopic hairs move food from all over the body surface to the mouth, using channels that can be seen on empty white shells. Short spines enable them to travel through the sand. A set of gills projects through the upper side of the shell in a five-rayed star pattern. Sand dollars are preyed upon by sunflower starfish (Figure 111). They typically cluster in large groups with no apparent reason for their location. One way to find them is to look during high tide from a dock or boat; then return to that spot during low tide.

Figure 117: The sea pen *(Ptilosarcus gurneyi)* is spectacular when expanded, as seen here in an aquarium, but you are more likely to see one appear as a bright orange disc level with the surface of the sand at low tide. It contracts and draws down into a burrow when exposed so that only its top shows. Sea pens occur at about the lowest tide level and extend into deeper water on many beaches in central Puget Sound, from Seattle to Bremerton. The sea pen is a colonial animal — a large number of miniature sea anemones organized around a calcified quill into a large ostrich plume affair. The colony has a sort of foot, which remains in a semipermanent burrow in the sand. Each individual in the colony is an individual filter feeder but has a gut cavity that connects to all the rest — true communal living! If observed in the dark, a relaxed and inflated sea pen can usually be stimulated to emit a greenish luminescence by touching or pinching it at either end. It is sometimes labeled in aquariums as *Leioptilus* or *Pennatula quadrangularis,* although these names are now technically obsolete.

Figure 118: The heart cockle *(Clinocardium nuttallii)* is a medium-sized bivalve with deep shells having small ribbing somewhat like that of scallops. The siphons (seen on the upper left of the shell in the photo) are short, so the shell is generally just below the surface of its typically sandy or sandy/mud habitat. Once you learn to see the fringed ends of its siphons at the surface of the sand, you can dig the heart cockle with your bare hands. Most often heart cockles are found when digging other clams, however, without any prior sign of their presence. There is not a lot of meat inside the shell, but some consider it very tasty in chowder; others think the taste too strong.

That shallow-burrowing habit of the heart cockle makes it vulnerable to predators such as skates and starfish. However, it is not defenseless. Starfish seem to have an odor that the heart cockle can detect at a distance of a few inches. When it senses danger, its long, sickle-shaped foot moves rapidly downward from between the gaping shells and pushes the whole cockle right up out of the sand. Additional thrusts with the foot continue until the cockle

sand dollar, sea pen, clam

117. **Expanded sea pen** *(Ptilosarcus gurneyi)*

118. **Heart cockle** *(Clinocardium nuttallii)*

116. **Sand dollars** *(Dendraster excentricus)*

Sandy, *Protected*

either fatigues or gets out of danger. The whole performance gives me the impression of a ludicrous Humpty Dumpty trying to ride a pogo stick. A number of snails, sea cucumbers, and scallops also have similarly vigorous escape responses in the presence of starfish.

The Eelgrass Habitat

Figure 119: Eelgrass is one of only a few flowering plants throughout the world that live in the sea. The other local one is surfgrass *(Phyllospadix)*, which occurs on exposed coastlines. The eelgrass illustrated *(Zostera marina)* is found extensively on protected sandy beaches in patches varying from a few square feet to huge beds. The roots tend to stabilize the sand. Sometimes mounds are formed when sand washes away around the edges, and additional sand is trapped in the roots. Eelgrass provides a habitat in which a variety of specially adapted animals can exist, some of which are shown in the following photos. Thus, eelgrass is interesting in itself and for the ecosystem it contains. It also is a source of food for Canada geese and a number of diving ducks.

119. Eelgrass *(Zostera marina)*, habitat for numerous species

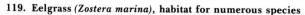

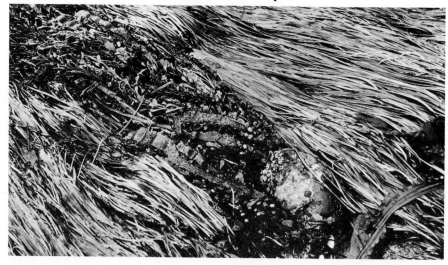

Figure 120: The brooding sea anemone *(Epiactis prolifera)* lives on blades of eelgrass, although it is sometimes found on other substrates, as seen here. It has two outstanding characteristics. As the name suggests, it buds new anemones from eggs which develop in a groove around the base of the tentacles; as these grow, they slowly move away — but meanwhile, the anemone looks like a brooding hen. Its other distinctive feature is a brightly striped color pattern of either green or red.

114

eelgrass, sea anemone, jellyfish

120. Brooding sea anemone *(Epiactis prolifera)*

121. Stalked jellyfish *(Haliclystus auricula)*

Figure 121: Another animal attached to eelgrass looks somewhat like a sea anemone but is actually an unusual, stalked jellyfish *(Haliclystus auricula)*. It has eight clusters of tentacles with stinging cells typical of jellyfish. The mouth faces upward, and if it is detached from the eelgrass, it is unable to swim like a normal jellyfish.

115

Sandy, *Protected*

122. Sea slug *(Phyllaplysia taylori)*

Lynwood S. Smith

123. Penpoint gunnel *(Apodichthys flavidus)*

Lynwood S. Smith

124. Hermit crab *(Paguristes turgidus)* in shell of hairy triton

116

Figure 122: One nudibranch *(Phyllaplysia taylori)* is camouflaged to somewhat match the width and striping of the eelgrass. It is found only on eelgrass, the larger ones only on eelgrass with wide blades. At a mature length of about one and one-half inches, it overhangs the edges of all but the widest eelgrass. This is most properly called a sea slug or tectibranch, since it has internal gills — located within the body cavity, which opens to the water through a slit on the side of the body. It is more closely related to the common garden slug than to typical nudibranchs (see Figure 32 for comparison).

Figure 123: The uncommon penpoint gunnel or blenny *(Apodichthys flavidus)* gets its name from a peculiar spine in a pocket at the front edge of the anal fin. The spine somewhat resembles the old-fashioned penpoints that required wooden holders and had to be dipped in ink bottles. This blenny's typical color is bright green, although several shades of yellow green are possible. Although eelgrass beds are its normal habitat, it is perhaps most commonly seen at public aquariums.

Figure 124: This hermit crab *(Paguristes turgidus)* is typical in most respects, except that it is usually found in eelgrass beds. The orange color is characteristic, and it may use a variety of snail shells to match its size (here it is using a hairy triton, *Fusitriton oregonensis*).

Sandy, *Protected*/**Muddy Sand,** *Protected*

125. Skeleton shrimp *(Caprella)*

Figure 125: The skeleton shrimp *(Caprella)* clings to eelgrass, seaweeds, hydroids (Figures 140, 141, 142), and any other convenient substrate in relatively protected water. Three pairs of posterior legs grasp the substrate, eggs are carried in a pouch in the middle of the skinny body, and the head end bears a pair of claws, which look and operate like those of the praying mantis. The skeleton shrimp sways from side to side snapping up tidbits that drift past. The name skeleton shrimp is a slight misnomer, since this animal is more closely related to sand hoppers than to shrimp. Its typical length of half an inch makes it hard to see at first, but you will notice the skeleton shrimp in a variety of places once you have first seen one.

Protected Muddy Sand Beaches – Examples and Species

Figure 126: The Skagit River in Washington deposits fine sediments on a sizable delta whose beaches are transitional — between typical sand and mud composition. This delta is also a special place for migratory waterfowl to rest and feed on eelgrass and an area for people to dig eastern soft-shell clams in an almost pure monoculture — there isn't much else there. This is one of the larger sandy mudflats in western Washington.

Figure 127: This photo shows the texture of the muddy sand and the shallow hole needed to obtain soft-shell clams. Eastern soft-shell clams *(Mya arenaria)* were probably introduced here from the Atlantic coast, where they are a mainstay of the seafood industry. Here they have only recently been dis-

118

126. **Clam diggers on sandy mudflat of Skagit River, Wa.**

127. **Opened eastern soft-shell clams**
(*Mya arenaria*), hinge visible

covered by recreational clam diggers and are not yet widely utilized. An uninitiated clam digger might first mistakenly identify them as small horse clams (Figure 108), but they are more oval than horse clams and have tannish rather than black skin on their siphon and around the edge of their very fragile shell. The final unique feature of the eastern soft-shell clam, and a sure identification, is seen after opening the shell and removing the meat: one of the shells has a little lip that crosses over into the other shell beneath the hinge. No other clam in Puget Sound has this feature. The Skagit tide flats support the largest local population of this clam, although it is widely distributed elsewhere, as well.

119

7
Mud beaches

Protected Mud Beaches – Examples and Species

Mud beaches occur in areas where a river enters a bay with a slow flow spreading out thinly over flat tidelands protected from wave action. If there were much current or wave action, the mud would be rapidly carried away — thus all mud beaches are protected beaches.

Most of the muddier beaches in the Puget Sound region occur at the back of long, narrow, protected bays. For the same reason that mud collects there, these bays have warm, quiet, organically rich waters in summer, a highly productive time for many organisms, not the least of which are oysters — especially when cultivated by man. Oysters thrive on the green "soup" of plankton, which is typical of these bays.

Bay View State Park near Anacortes, Washington, is a moderately sandy mud beach with large beds of eelgrass offshore. Some areas have been filled with material dredged from the bay, leaving a mostly sandy beach; further out, however, the toe-to-ankle-deep mud has not been disturbed by man. There are accumulations of dead eelgrass which will decay and, although it is a bit smelly at times, will further contribute to making fine, rich mud again. The bay is large and open, faces north, and is protected from the winter storms.

Some of the muddier beaches in Puget Sound include Belfair State Park at the end of Hood Canal, Liberty Bay (Figure 128) near Poulsbo, and all of the bays between Olympia and Shelton. Commercial oyster growers in these areas alter the environment by solidifying the mud with an overlay of gravel. They also often dike their land by erecting perimeter walls so that water can cover all of the oysters, protecting them from excessive heat in summer and from freezing in winter when the tide is out. Most oyster dikes are private property, but there is some public oyster land on the west shore of Hood

Mud, *Protected*

129. Footprints in soft mud, Liberty Bay

128. Protected mud beach at Liberty Bay near Poulsbo, Wa.

122

Canal, particularly on the delta of the Dosewallips River. Remnants of oyster dikes can also be seen at Belfair State Park.

Muddy environments can occur in surprising places. Sucia Island in the San Juans is usually considered rocky, but Fossil Bay, at the island's southeastern edge, has only rocky sides — the bottom is mud. The mud probably originates from the winter floods of the Fraser River (its mouth is at Vancouver, British Columbia) and is augmented by decaying kelp that blankets the bottom. There are similarly isolated pockets of mud elsewhere in the San Juan and Gulf islands. In British Columbia, the waters of the Strait of Georgia are somewhat warmer than those of Puget Sound and the San Juans, so oysters seed there naturally during most years and are then found on *rocky* beaches rather than those associated with mud. On the Dosewallips River delta, the muddiest parts are high up on the beach among clumps and islands of marsh grass, which protect the mud from erosion by waves and currents. Given a thousand years or so of continued deposition of mud, this area will be basically terrestrial, rather than marine.

Figure 128: Liberty Bay near Poulsbo is typical of quiet, protected mud bays, although the water here probably is not as warm as in the southernmost bays of Puget Sound. The mud is firm enough to walk on and to support oysters — no dikes are needed. The poles serve as boundary markers for property owners and also permit accurate moorage of barges or skiffs at high tide for easy loading and unloading of oysters at low tide.

Figure 129: Not all of Liberty Bay mud is firm enough to walk on. These footprints illustrate a basic fact of life about mud, whether for man or seashore animals — it is difficult to stay on its surface. Animals on a mud beach must be able to move around in it, breath in it, feed in it. In spite of its organic richness, the greatest number of organisms that live here are microscopic; burrowing worms and a few clams constitute most of the remainder. Thus, mudflats at low tide, even though teeming with life, look pretty barren to the unappreciative eye. Given any kind of hard, stable surface, however — a rare rock, a gravel beach, a piling, dock, or an oyster dike — and all sorts of lovely things take hold and grow vigorously.

Mud, *Protected*

Figure 130: Oyster farming's major crop today is the Pacific or Japanese oyster *(Crassostrea gigas),* originally imported many years ago as tiny young oysters attached to old oyster shells. The oysters in the picture are two and one-half to three inches long and have completed three years of growth. Even though they are resting on a gravel bottom inside a dike, the silting influence of the surrounding mud is evident. Excessive silting could suffocate them.

Figure 131: The native or Olympia oyster *(Ostrea lurida)* is nowhere nearly as abundant as it once was but is still famous as a gastronomic delicacy. Its cultivation in Oyster Bay near Olympia, Washington, keeps it seeding naturally in adjoining areas around Olympia. There are other scattered populations near Victoria and Vancouver, British Columbia, as well as occasional specimens up and down the Pacific coast from northern British Columbia to Baja California. The shells are gray and about the size of a silver dollar when mature.

Encrusted around the oysters in the picture is a gelatinous mass of colonial tunicates, similar to those found on the outer coast (Figure 39). These tunicates filter their food out of the water as do the oysters. Thus, mud bays with their pea green plankton blooms in the summer are great places for the tunicates, as long as they can stay out of the mud. Pictured is probably a species of *Amaroucium,* but microscopic examination is necessary for certain identification.

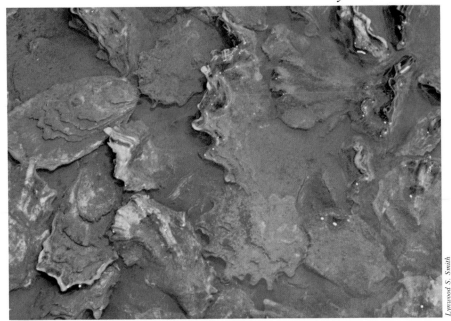

130. Pacific or Japanese oyster *(Crassostrea gigas)*

131. Native or Olympia oyster *(Ostrea lurida),* encrusted with colonial tunicates

125

Mud, *Protected*

132. Hairy sea squirt *(Boltenia villosa)*

133. Japanese oyster drills *(Ocenebra japonica)*

Figure 132: Not all tunicates are colonial. Some are solitary like this hairy sea squirt *(Boltenia villosa)*. It hangs from a very tough stalk, attaches to any kind of solid substrate, and can be found on a wide variety of rocky beaches, on floats, and on oyster dikes. It starts out life as a free-swimming tadpolelike creature but soon cements its head to something solid and loses its tail. The gill cavity enlarges to form a bulge at the end of the stalk, which serves to filter food; an intake and outlet opening channels water through. If you squeeze the bulge, water squirts out of these openings; hence the name sea squirt. The name "tunicate" is derived from its tough outer coat or "tunic."

Figure 133: What weeds are to the farmer, oyster predators are to the oysterman. The worst of these is a snail, the Japanese oyster drill *(Ocenebra japonica)*. Like the moon snail (Figure 83), it uses its radula (Figure 38) to rasp a hole through the oyster's shell to eat it. Oyster drills were unknowingly imported into the Pacific Northwest with Japanese oyster seed many years ago. They are controlled by hand-picking them from the oyster beds and inspecting all oysters being moved into areas that are still drill-free. Poison would be easier, but oysters and drills are both mollusks and so similar that any poison tried thus far kills the oysters as well as the drills.

For a contrast to the oyster drill, look at a whelk *(Thais lamellosa,* Figure 48). The *Thais* shell grows smooth in areas where the water is calm and frilly where wave action is strong. Thus, whelks in oyster areas are not usually confused with oyster drills. The egg cases of oyster drills are readily confused with those of several whelks, until you have seen both. Their general shape is similar, but those of the oyster drill have strongly curved sides and the top is tipped over. The whelk's egg cases are more erect and round like a vase.

Figure 134: The hole in the clamshell is a sample of the oyster drill's handiwork with its radula (Figure 38). Moon snails (Figure 83) drill similar holes.

134. Clamshell with hole bored by oyster drill

127

Mud, *Protected*

Figure 135: Without being directly harmful, the problems that the slipper snail *(Crepidula fornicata)* creates is graphically illustrated here. Slipper snails normally cling, almost permanently, to a firm surface — a dike wall, another slipper shell (stacks of slipper shells are common), an oyster shell, or as here, a whelk. In this photograph, when the tide went out and left the snail hanging, the whelk had to support another shell besides its own and obviously has found this a fatiguing situation. The foot muscles are slowly stretching, and if the low tide lasts too long, the whelk will fall, which may or may not be a problem, depending on what is below. Falling into soft mud, for example, could be fatal for all concerned.

Figure 136: The green shore crab *(Hemigrapsus oregonensis)* looks very similar to the purple shore crab (Figure 63) except that it is green, has hairs on top of its walking legs, and tolerates more mud than its purple relative. The green shore crab likes a variety of habitats — sand, gravel, or even rocky beaches that have a little mud present. It can sometimes be found on the same beach as the purple shore crab, and during some years a multitude of green shore crabs inhabit oyster dikes.

The green shore crab sometimes ventures out onto the soft mud beside the oyster dike, half-swimming, half-walking in this difficult medium. This is a bigger feat than one might realize — fine mud can clog gills, cover sensory organs, overwhelm the food-sorting and water-pumping appendages, and generally make life strenuous. By comparison, a person would sink waist-deep to chest-deep in this mud and be almost helpless.

Figure 137: Another crab that prefers a firm muddy substrate and frequently occurs in oyster dikes is the graceful cancer crab *(Cancer gracilis)*. While catching this crab is not regulated in Washington, it rarely grows to more than about four inches in length across the shell and is therefore hardly large enough to bother taking home to eat. Further, the legs and claws, thin and weak compared to either Dungeness or red crabs, contain less meat than crabs of comparable size. For identification, in addition to the small legs and claws, the shape of the notches on the front edge of the shell is distinctive, and the light red color with a slight purple cast is typical.

snail, crab

Lynwood S. Smith

135. Slipper snail
(Crepidula fornicata)
hanging onto a tiring whelk

136. Green shore crab *(Hemigrapsus oregonensis)*

137. Graceful cancer crab *(Cancer gracilis)*

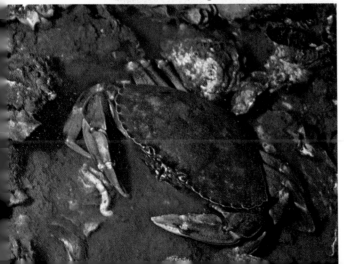

129

Floats
sea anemone

Figure 138: If I were to choose one specimen guaranteed to be found on almost any float in the Pacific Northwest, it would be the sun anemone *(Metridium senile)*. This marine animal grows prolifically, in sizes up to eighteen inches tall. Its tentacles are finely divided, the fineness varying with the several subspecies. It occurs in a variety of colors — white, tan, light gray — with white being most common. If you are setting up a seawater aquarium, you can peel the surprisingly hardy anemone off its substrate with a blunt edge (fingernails are fine); it will reattach if left undisturbed overnight. It can also crawl along very slowly on its foot and may leave fragments of it behind. These fragments grow into tiny new anemones in a form of asexual reproduction. Sun anemones feed on small animals that drift by in the water currents.

138. Sun anemones *(Metridium senile)*

Floats

Lynwood S. Smith

139. Sea blubber *(Cyanea capillata)*, center, and
    sea anemones *(Tealia)*, left and right

140. Hydroid

132

Figure 139: Sea anemones, *Tealia* (seen on left and right of photo), are common on floats. Their tentacles are heavy like most anemones', but their coloring is distinctive. Compare them to the related species of *Tealia* shown in Figure 68, which has red stripes on its body instead of a uniform color.

Many species of jellyfish accumulate around floats, more because the floats obstruct their passage than from a desire to stay there. Jellyfish are fun to observe and touch. All jellyfishes in Puget Sound are harmless *except the one pictured* (in the center) — the sea blubber *(Cyanea capillata).* The clear or whitish, saucer-shaped part of the body is usually uppermost, with the frilly mouthparts and tentacles (orange, red, or brown) streaming out below. The jellyfish pictured is on its side and crowded up against a float by the current. Stinging cells on its long streamers are strong enough to inject poison through human skin and give a burning sensation. The poison is not fatal, but with repeated stinging, some people become hyperallergic to it, in which case the sting can be fatal. This problem is greatest in summer when the water is warmest, and the jellyfish has grown to its largest size — up to two feet across with five- to six-foot tentacles. This is the most likely time for someone to swim unknowingly through the tentacles and be extensively stung. While the jellyfish just drifts and cannot actively hunt for prey, neither can it get out of your way. It is also caught in fishermen's nets in great numbers and the severed tentacles can still give a full-strength sting. More than one commercial fisherman has had to change his occupation because of an allergy to jellyfish.

Some potent jellyfishes found much farther south occasionally drift north and wash up on our coastal beaches in surprisingly large numbers. These include the Portuguese man-o-war, *(Physalia),* with pear-shaped, gas-filled floats about the size of a nickel; and the sail jellyfish *(Velella),* a little purple disc as big as a silver dollar with a small vertical fin across the middle.

Figure 140: Other predictable residents of floats include a great number of species collectively called hydroids. Although they look like plants at first, they are actually colonial animals related to sea anemones. Careful observation shows that while most of the structure is brown and opaque, the tips of the branches are a translucent white. These white tips are miniature anemones. With a little persistence, it should be easy to find a dozen or more kinds of hydroids on even a halfway productive series of floats. This one probably belongs to the genus *Obelia,* but the species is not readily determined without magnification.

Floats

Figure 141: Another distinctive, although not so common hydroid is the ostrich plume hydroid, *Aglaophenia* (species not readily determined). Its featherlike fronds are three inches long at maximum and each branch on the frond carries several dozen feeding organs. The heavy structures between the branches are reproductive bodies. In addition to floats, ostrich plume hydroids can be found on rocks and other solid substrates.

Figure 142: Hydroids have a jellyfish stage as well as a sessile stage seen in Figure 141. A large hydroid jellyfish is the water jellyfish *(Aequorea aequorea)*. This jellyfish has stinging cells similar to the sea blubber, but the cells rarely penetrate human skin; thus, for most people it is harmless. It has a thick, almost rigid body up to four inches in diameter with a clear center (no radial lines). There is no guarantee you will see such jellyfish around floats, since it drifts far and wide.

141. Ostrich plume hydroid *(Aglaophenia)*

142. Water jellyfish *(Aequorea aequorea)*

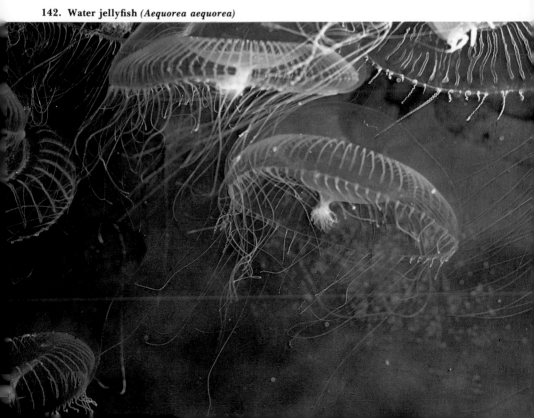

Floats

Figure 143: The name thimble jellyfish describes both the size and the shape of *Coryne (Sarsia) rosaria.* The red structure hanging inside the bell has a mouth opening at the lower end. The red substance is composed of gonadal material, which you would see only when the jellyfish is sexually mature. By jellyfish population standards, this one is very common, but you still won't see one every day you go looking for it.

Figure 144: You may also see a nickel-sized sphere zooming around floats, trailing two streamers behind it. This is the sea gooseberry, *Pleurobrachia,* which looks like a jellyfish but belongs to a related group, the comb jellies. Its two streamers are "fishing lines" with which the sphere catches plankton animals. The streamers retract up to the sphere to deliver the catch to the mouth, which is in the center underneath the sphere. The sea gooseberry is propelled by eight longitudinal rows of "combs" that beat in a coordinated fashion.

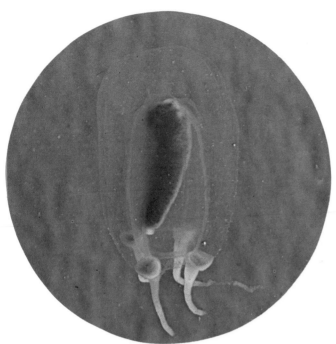

143. Thimble jellyfish *(Coryne (Sarsia) rosaria)*

144. Sea gooseberries *(Pleurobrachia)*, a comb jelly

Floats

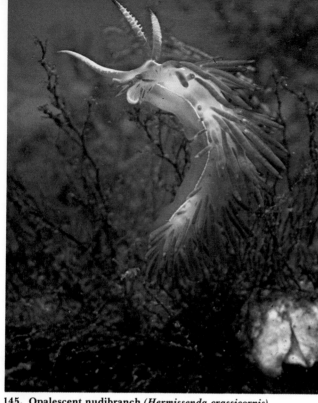

145. Opalescent nudibranch *(Hermissenda crassicornis)*

146. Bread crumb sponge

Lynwood S. Smith

147. Feather-duster worms

138

Figure 145: Wherever there are hydroids, you are also likely to find the opalescent nudibranch *(Hermissenda crassicornis)*. With its fluorescent orange plumes and white pinstriping, it must be rated among the more spectacular nudibranchs. It is found around hydroids because it eats them — simply crawls up the stalk, slurps in the polyp on the end, and nips it off the stem. The stinging cells from the hydroid pass through the nudibranch's digestive tract unharmed and end up in the plumes, where they remain functional.

Figure 146: Sponges are colonial animals in which simple cells build urn-shaped, external skeletons from glass (silica), limestone, or flexible protein. Sponges of more complex shape (any of several species of *Halichondria* and *Haliclona*) form an irregular encrustation over considerable area. Colors are extremely variable; they may be gray, amethyst, or lavender, although the yellow-tan-brown series is more common. Basically composed of silica, the pictured sponge crumbles like wet bread when touched or handled very much, leading to the name bread crumb sponge.

Figure 147: The most conspicuous worms on floats — the feather-duster worms — live in tough, leathery tubes and have feathery heads, which they withdraw into their tubes in reaction to any disturbance or sometimes even a passing shadow. Their plumelike finery leads several species to be lumped together under the name feather-duster worms. Although related to other segmented worms like the pile worm (Figure 87) or the earthworm, the feather-duster worm is more specialized than either by virtue of its fancy plumes, which are feeding structures, and a special collar around the base of the plumes, which produces the tube. There are short bristles along the body which grip the tube and make it impossible to pull the worm out — split the tube open carefully if you have to see the whole worm (otherwise leave it alone). There are two easily recognized groups of feather-duster worms: one with branched plumes *(Schizobranchia)* and one with unbranched plumes *(Eudistylia)*. Their colors range from almost white to rich dark reds and purples.

Floats, *Worm*

Figure 148: If you get a chance to do so without damaging private property, look inside old logs along the beach or where floats have been abandoned. If the wood crumbles away and reveals a myriad of tunnels, you are looking at the handiwork of one of two borers: a little white isopod, *Limnoria,* or the shipworm, *Teredo* (also an isopod), which is shown here. Although the shipworm rarely makes holes over one-quarter inch in diameter, it may bore holes up to three-quarters inch in diameter. The shipworm is actually not a worm, but a bivalve with two tiny shells used as boring tools, a long, fleshy body, and a sort of feather-shaped calcareous appendage at its posterior end. The shipworm eats some wood, an unusual diet, since few animals have the proper enzymes to utilize wood. It also feeds on material filtered out of the respiratory water it circulates through its burrow.

148. Shipworm *(Teredo)*

140

Appendix 1
Basic preparation of seafoods

The first rule in preparing food from the seashore is to deal with it quickly. Both fish and shellfish contain high levels of polyunsaturated fats, which can deteriorate more rapidly than almost any other kind of food. Keep the food animals alive or cool or both until you are ready to cook them.

Steamer Clams

These are the littlenecks and small butter clams. If possible, let them sit in a container of cool seawater for a few hours or hang them in seawater in a burlap bag from the side of a dock or boat to allow them to clean out any sand inside their shells. Then wash them to remove sand from the outside of the shells. Check especially for dead, sand-filled shells — some of these can be extremely deceptive, and it takes only one to ruin an entire pot of steamers. Also discard any clams that have died and gaped open. Put the remainder in a container of appropriate size with an inch or so of tap water in the bottom. Steam (boil) them, usually for two to four minutes, until they all open.

Most people scoop steamer clams out of the shell, dip them in melted butter, and eat them whole. Small clams are better for eating whole. The liquid in the bottom of the pan, clam nectar, makes a fine hot drink, either plain or spiced to suit your taste.

Large Butter Clams

Wash the clams and remove any obvious sand from the outside. Insert a thin-bladed knife between the shells where there is a slight gap (the siphon end) and cut the muscles which hold the shell shut. The muscles are close to each end; once you find them, it becomes a simple job. After you cut the muscles at one end, it is usually easier to get at the muscles at the other end. Many people then cut away dark-colored parts of the clam and wash out any further sand under cold running water. Usually the clams are put through a meat grinder for use in chowder.

Don't be surprised if you find a small crab inside the clamshell — it is a common hitchhiker in most larger clams and causes no harm. Also, don't be concerned about a clear, plasticlike rod which may pop out of the stomach region when you cut into it. This is a normal part of the digestive system, not a parasite.

Razor Clams

Razor clams are certain to be sandy, and most do not live long enough after capture to make self-cleaning practical. Be prepared to keep them cool while

141

you carry them to a convenient cleaning site. There are two ways to remove the clam from its shell: cut it out, as above, or dip it in hot (not quite boiling) water until the shell separates from the meat. The hot water method is faster and assists in washing out the sand. In either case, you then split open the clam lengthwise with scissors or a knife, remove the gills, and thoroughly massage the clam under cold running water to remove any sand remaining in crevices and cavities.

Razor clams are normally laid out flat, breaded if you like, and fried quickly in a hot pan. If tough, they are more likely overcooked than undercooked — a minute or two of frying on each side is usually sufficient.

Horse Clams and Gweducs

These differ from razor clams in only minor respects. Both have a thin, leathery skin on the siphon which is most easily removed after dipping the clam in hot (almost boiling) water for about one minute. The horse clams are then cleaned (removing all the dark-colored parts) and commonly ground up for chowder, while the gweducs may be fried, although the siphon, split and laid out flat, usually requires some tenderizing by a little pounding.

Other Clams, Mussels

There are many small clams in the Northwest's beaches, few of which get utilized, sometimes for good reason. The bent-nose clam and its close relatives are among these because they are almost always sandy, the siphons are small, and there is not much other meat.

The heart cockle is prized by some people. The shells close along a corrugated line, so opening with heat is easier than by using a knife. It has a short siphon but a large foot. The flavor is stronger and the meat tougher than most clams, so it is typically ground up for chowder.

The eastern soft-shell should be treated like a small gweduc or horse clam. Increasingly appreciated in the Northwest, where it has been introduced, it is one of the primary commercial clams on the Atlantic coast.

There are two mussels to consider — the California mussel of the outer coast and the small bay mussel of protected waters. In both cases the potential problem is red tide — mussels seem to be particularly susceptible to accumulating any toxic organisms present, and eating a batch of "loaded" mussels can be fatal to humans, even though the organism does not harm the mussel. Oysters and butter clams can also be affected by red tides, but razor clams are rarely toxic. Red tides may occur at any time during the summer months, even though the water may not actually appear red, so don't take chances just because the water "looks all right." Toxic red tides do not occur in Hood Canal, Puget Sound, or the Strait of Georgia, although there are some nontoxic plankton blooms there which appear reddish. When in doubt, contact your local fisheries representative.

142

Prepare mussels like steamer clams. Clean the outside of the shells and steam them until they open. The large mussels can be eaten with a spoon. They are particularly tasty in spring when the ovaries are filled with bright orange eggs. The little mussels can be pulled out of their shells using the tough inedible threads with which they were formerly attached to the rocks. They can also be used in a seafood stew, shell and all.

Oysters

Washington state recently passed a law requiring that oyster shells be left on the beach as places for new oysters to "set," so be prepared to clean them on the spot. While it is possible to open them with heat, the most workable way on the beach is with an oyster knife, a stiff-bladed knife sharpened mostly on the rounded tip. You can purchase it inexpensively at most sporting goods stores. There are two schools of thought on how to use the knife. In either case, the problem is to cut the muscle that holds the shells closed. It is located about two-thirds of the way from the hinge end going towards the wide end of the shells, approximately in the middle of its width. One school inserts the knife at the side of the shell opposite the muscle, keeping the tip of the blade against the upper (flatter) shell and moving it back and forth until the muscle is severed and the shell pops open because of the hinge's elasticity. The other school goes through the upper shell close to the end, away from the hinge where the shell is thin, and then slides the blade along the lower shell until the muscle is cut. In either case, the idea is not to slice up the oyster — or your finger! Keep the shelled oysters in a cooled, clean container. You can eat the small ones raw, dipped in a seafood sauce. No further preparation is needed before cooking, but you can dip them in flour or breading first. Most cookbooks have a variety of recipes.

Crabs

All species of crabs are handled much the same. Keep them alive until they are cooked to guarantee that they have not spoiled. Most commonly, the crab is put into boiling seawater alive and left for twenty minutes after the water returns to a rolling boil. If the apparently reflexive, brief thrashing bothers you, put the crab in cold *fresh water,* then start heating it. The warming fresh water seems to anesthetize it. You can also strike the crab a sharp blow on the center of the underside of the body, killing it by stunning the nervous system (which is ventral rather than dorsal as in vertebrates). Then remove the back of the crab and clean out the internal organs, cooking only the meat-containing parts for twenty minutes. Cooking the whole crab is reputed to retain all the rich oils and other flavors present in the internal organs, while the other method results in only the pure flavor of the meat. I have tried it both ways and find that the two methods produce slightly different flavors, but you should try them for yourself.

143

Other Seashore Animals

Open either *scallops* or *rock scallops* the way you open oysters; the muscle is in about the same location. The muscle is all that is normally eaten of scallops. It makes up nearly half of the fleshy part of larger ones.

In *abalone,* the foot and the stemlike part that anchors it to the shell are edible. Clean off everything except the white meat. To tenderize it, give it a few taps with a steak hammer or the side of a meat cleaver until the meat goes limp.

Octopus can be quite tough unless properly prepared. The edible portions are the arms and the muscular bag around the internal organs. Discard the head (eyes, beak, cartilaginous brain case) and the internal organs (gills, hearts, gonads, digestive tract). It is easier to remove the skin after partial cooking, although skinning it when fresh is not really difficult. The sheet of muscle around the body is somewhat tender after about forty-five minutes of boiling, more tender if cooked in a pressure cooker. The arms are tougher and can also be put in a pressure cooker. However, I believe the easiest method of preparation is to freeze the arms, skin, suckers, and all. When ready to cook them, cut the arms into two- to three-inch-long cylinders. Stand each cylinder on end and pare off the skin, suckers, and especially a tough white sheath around the muscle itself. Then pound the end of the remaining white cylinder, still frozen, into a quarter-inch-thick patty. By then, the ice crystals will have broken the tough fibers. Fried in butter, such patties are fork tender.

Sea urchin eggs are delicacies in many European and South American countries. Simply break open the shell and remove the five orange ovaries, which are shaped something like grapefruit sections. Eat them raw or marinated in a hot sauce or onion sauce. The testes are the same shape, but gray in color; they are usually discarded because of their slightly bitter taste (from iodine content).

The California *sea cucumber* has five large muscles running lengthwise inside the body cavity. Split the cucumber open lengthwise, peel out the muscles, and wash off any remaining slime. Blanch the muscles in hot water for two to three minutes, then fry them in butter. The flavor is somewhere between frog legs and crab, but it is a lot of work for a little meat.

Snails have never been popular locally, although I have seen an occasional moon snail shell in the old shell piles from Indian potlatches. *Whelks* are also supposed to be edible, but I have not tried them.

Kelp

Kelp, several species of large, heavy, brown seaweed, is a regular part of the diet only in Asian countries. However, *Sunset Magazine* published a recipe in 1973 for cutting into rings and pickling hollow stalks of seal head kelp *(Nereocystis)*. If interested, inquire about it from the magazine.

Appendix 2
Public aquariums in the Pacific Northwest

Public aquariums offer an attractive family outing, especially when it is impossible to go to the beach. Most provide an excellent cross-section of local species as well as the exotic and spectacular animals that they advertise.

The following list describes aquariums in British Columbia, Washington, and Oregon.

Vancouver, British Columbia

The Vancouver Aquarium is among the three largest marine aquariums in North America. Located in Stanley Park, Vancouver, it features fine marine mammal displays (killer whale, beluga whale, white-sided dolphin, seal, sea otter), plus a superb variety of smaller marine life including fishes and invertebrates of British Columbia and the tropics. There is an excellent bookstore and educational program associated with this aquarium.

Victoria, British Columbia

Sealand of the Pacific features marine life of the Pacific Northwest, including most fish species found in the area. Underwater displays are viewed through large windows, while on the upper deck performing seals and sea lions are on display. The main attraction is a killer whale show.

At the Pacific Undersea Gardens Ltd., visitors observe marine life from a viewing chamber beneath the surface of the Pacific Ocean. A performance-oriented aquarium, it features diving shows and native marine life including a performing giant Pacific octopus.

145

Seattle, Washington

The Seattle Marine Aquarium is on the downtown waterfront at the outer end of Pier 56 and describes itself as the original home of the killer whale. The aquarium features a number of shows involving seals, whales, and dolphins, and also exhibits harbor seals. Small tanks display an excellent variety of local sea life. One open shallow tank has a sign "Please Touch — Gently," so that kids of all ages can more personally experience some of the hardier specimens.

The Seattle Aquarium, municipally owned and operated, will open in the fall of 1976. Located beside Pier 59 in a new complex built over Elliott Bay, the aquarium will display Puget Sound marine animals in walk-through exhibits of typical habitats of the Sound — a sandy beach, a mudflat/estuary, and a rocky coast. The visitor will also be able to witness plants and animals of the Sound through a glass-enclosed underwater viewing room. Harbor seals, northern fur seals, and sea otters will be exhibited in the marine mammal complex. Other features will include a working salmon hatchery, a salmon ladder, and educational exhibits on principles of survival, man's relationship to the sea, and freshwater habitats.

Tacoma, Washington

The Point Defiance Aquarium in Point Defiance Park is the result of an enthusiastically supported bond issue. In its newest quarters this excellent aquarium has outdoor pools for porpoises, harbor seals, and sea otters. A 135,000-gallon community tank displays many of the larger species in near-natural surroundings. The aquarium features the octopus and supplies other aquariums with this species.

Westport, Washington

The Westport Aquarium, open April through October, specializes in northern Pacific sea life, such as large octopus, wolf-eel, and sea anemones, as well as trained harbor seals. Although relatively small, it is worth the low price of a visit if you are in the area.

Seaside, Oregon

The Seaside Aquarium, privately owned, opened in 1937. It houses thirty-five tanks of invertebrates and fishes, and is especially proud of its sea anemone collection. Its colony of harbor seals was born and raised there, the oldest being thirty-one years old.

Depoe Bay, Oregon

In continuous operation since 1928, the Aquarium is one of the oldest in the United States. This small aquarium is the home of a thirty-two-year-old seal, expected to give birth this July. Aside from ten performing seals, the aquarium displays examples of local tide pool and other marine species.

Newport, Oregon

On the campus of Oregon State University, the Marine Science Center houses an aquarium-museum, auditorium, and other public facilities. Marine fishes and invertebrates native to the shores and coastal waters of Oregon are displayed in an 11,000-gallon aquarium. Other native marine forms are in tanks arranged to show the animals' natural habitat. It also has a handling pool where visitors may closely examine intertidal animals. During summer months the Science Center features a SEATAUQUA program, offering a variety of educational opportunities to the public. Programs include illustrated talks, films, shoreline nature hikes, and a spectrum of marine-related short courses.

Oregon Undersea Gardens, Inc. displays over 5,000 sea life specimens (tube worms, Pacific salmon, wolf-eels, an octopus) in an approximation of their natural habitats. Visitors are permitted to pick up and examine intertidal animals such as starfish, sea anemones, sea cucumbers, hermit crabs, chitons, and snails in the "touch and feel" tank. It also features a show with scuba divers.

Appendix 3
Regulatory agencies

Many of the regulations concerning the use of the seashore and its resources can be found in free pamphlets at local hardware and sporting goods stores. Most major cities have a branch of the appropriate agency. Even in outlying areas, the local telephone directory may list a fisheries patrol officer or fisheries warden who can be helpful. If you still have questions, write the regulatory agencies listed below.

National Agencies – Regional Offices

CANADA

Department of the Environment
Fisheries and Marine Service
1090 West Pender Street
Vancouver 1, British Columbia, Canada

UNITED STATES

United States Fish and Wildlife Service
Division of Law Enforcement
Pacific Region
P.O. Box 3737
Portland, Oregon 97208
(enforces federal fish and wildlife laws in Washington, Oregon, Idaho, and Hawaii)

United States Fish and Wildlife Service
Division of Law Enforcement
2800 Cottage Way
Room E-1924
Sacramento, California 95825
(enforces federal laws in California and Nevada)

Law Enforcement and Marine Mammal Protection Division
National Marine Fisheries Service
1700 Westlake Avenue North
Seattle, Washington 98109
(covers Washington, Oregon, Colorado, Montana, Utah, Idaho, North and South Dakota, and Wyoming)

Law Enforcement and Marine Mammal Protection Division
National Marine Fisheries Service
300 South Ferry Street
Terminal Island, California 90731
(covers California, Nevada, Arizona, New Mexico, and Hawaii)

State or Provincial Agencies – Main Offices

BRITISH COLUMBIA

Fish and Wildlife Branch
Department of Recreation and Conservation
4529 Canada Way
Burnaby, British Columbia, Canada

WASHINGTON

Department of Fisheries
115 General Administration Building
Olympia, Washington 98504

OREGON

Fish Commission of Oregon
307 State Office Building
1400 S.W. Fifth Avenue
Portland, Oregon 97201

CALIFORNIA

Department of Fish and Game
Resources Building
1416 Ninth Street
Sacramento, California 95814

Appendix 4
Further reading

General books about seashore life are numerous. You can consult with your local bookstore or librarian to make selections. The following list includes books specifically about the Pacific Northwest, which you might not otherwise find.

Carl, G. Clifford. 1971. *Some Common Marine Fishes of British Columbia.* Handbook no. 23. Victoria, B. C.: British Columbia Provincial Museum, Department of Recreation and Conservation. The Provincial Museum in Victoria, B. C., publishes a series of inexpensive, authoritative handbooks on several groups of marine animals, available at public aquariums and larger bookstores.

Griffith, Lela M. 1967. *Intertidal Univalves of British Columbia.* Handbook no. 26. Victoria, B. C.: British Columbia Provincial Museum. See note above on Carl, G. Clifford.

Guberlet, Muriel L. 1956. *Seaweeds at Ebb Tide.* Seattle: Univ. of Washington Press. This book identifies and illustrates with black-and-white drawings most common seaweeds and kelps on seashores in this area.

Hart, John Lawson. 1973. *Pacific Fishes of Canada.* Bulletin no. 180. Ottawa, Ontario: Fisheries Research Board of Canada. This is the authoritative source for identification of marine and migratory fishes. Each species is described in detail and illustrated, a few of them in color.

Kozloff, Eugene N. 1973. *Seashore Life of Puget Sound, the Strait of Georgia, and the San Juan Archipelago.* Seattle: Univ. of Washington Press. This is a recent compilation of local marine species, describing their identification and biology in the traditional zoological fashion — phylum by phylum (coelenterates, annelids, echinoderms, etc.).

Kozloff, Eugene N. 1974. *Keys to the Marine Invertebrates of Puget Sound, the San Juan Archipelago, and Adjacent Regions.* Seattle: Univ. of Washington Press. This is the authoritative source for the *technical* identification of most species of seashore animals in the area.

Quayle, D. B. 1960. *The Intertidal Bivalves of British Columbia.* Handbook no. 17. Victoria, B. C.: British Columbia Provincial Museum. See note for Carl, G. Clifford.

Rice, Thomas C. 1972. *Marine Shells of the Pacific Northwest.* Revised ed. Edmonds, Wa.: Ellis Robinson Publishing Co. This is an inexpensive handbook for shell collectors showing all the chitons, snails, and clams of the region, illustrated in color.

Scagel, Robert F. 1971. *Guide to Common Seaweeds of British Columbia.* Handbook no. 27. Victoria, B.C.: British Columbia Provincial Museum, Department of Recreation and Conservation. This is similar to Guberlet 1956 above, but less expensive.

Smith, Lynwood S. 1962. *Common Seashore Life of the Pacific Northwest.* Healdsburg, Ca.: Naturegraph Co. This is also a traditional, taxonomic approach to seashore animals, similar to Kozloff 1973, but less comprehensive and less expensive. Intended for the complete novice to seashore biology.

Table 1

Geographical Distribution of Species Listed in this Book

Key: *** = abundant ** =common * = occasional blank = rare or absent

Figure	Species	Outer Coast Sandy	Outer Coast Rocky	Strait of Juan de Fuca	San Juan Islands	Hood Canal	Puget Sound North/South	
29, 30	ABALONE		*	*	*			
	BARNACLES							
47	Acorn	***	***	***	***	***	***	***
16	Goose	*	***	*	*			
17, 49	Ribbed	*	***	***	***	**	**	*
	CHITONS							
24	Leather		**	**	**	*	*	*
35	Lined		**	**	**	*	*	
36, 37	Moccasin		**	**	**	*	*	
34	Mossy		**	**	**	**	**	
	CLAMS, Similar Bivalves							
81	Bent-nose			*	*	*	*	*
81, 82	Butter				*	**	**	**
127	Eastern soft-shell				*	*	*	*
106, 107	Gweduc			*	*	*	*	*
118	Heart cockle			*	*	**	**	**
108	Horse				*	**	**	**
82	Macoma				*	**	**	**
82	Manila littleneck					***	**	**
81	Native littleneck			*	**	**	**	**
75	Piddock		**	*	*	*	*	
97	Razor	***						
	CRABS							
65	Black-clawed shore		*	*	*	*	*	
66	Decorator		*	*	*	*	*	*
103	Dungeness	**	*	**	*	**	**	*
137	Graceful cancer						*	*
136	Green shore				*	**	**	**
64	Hairy cancer		*	*	*	*	*	
67	Kelp		*	*	*	*	*	
42	Porcelain		**	**	*	*	*	
63	Purple shore		*	**	**	***	***	**
104, 105	Red (rock)			*	*	**	**	
	FISH							
43, 44	Clingfish		*	*	*		*	
77	Cockscomb prickleback		*	*	*	*	*	
123	Penpoint gunnel (blenny)		*	*	*	*	*	*
94, 95	Tide pool sculpin		**	**	**	**	**	**
22, 89, 90, 124	HERMIT CRABS		*	*	**	**	**	*

Figure	Species	Outer Coast Sandy	Outer Coast Rocky	Strait of Juan de Fuca	San Juan Islands	Hood Canal	Puget Sound North/South
140, 141	HYDROIDS		★	★	★	★	★	★
	JELLYFISH						
139	Sea blubber			★	★	★	★	★
144	Sea gooseberry (comb jelly)	★	★	★	★	★	★
121	Stalked				★	★	★
143	Thimble			★	★★	★	★
142	Water			★	★★	★	★
	KELP						
15	Sea Palm		★				
46	Seal head (bladder)	★★	★★	★★	★★	★★	★
	MUSSELS						
49	Bay		★	★★	★★★	★★★	★★★	★★★
17	California	★★★	★★	★			
	NUDIBRANCHS						
70	*Cadlina*		★	★	★	★	★
72	*Dendronotus*		★	★	★		
114	Frosted				★	★	★	★
145	Opalescent		★	★	★	★	★	★
122	*Phyllaplysia* (sea slug)			★	★		
33	Red		★	★			
69	Sea lemon		★	★	★	★	★
32	Spotted (ringed)		★	★	★		
71	*Triopha*			★	★		
78	OCTOPUS		★	★	★	★	★	★
	OYSTERS						
131	Native (Olympia)						★
130	Pacific (Japanese) (Willapa Harbor)	★			★★	★	★★★
58	Rock (jingle shell)		★	★	★	★	★
116	SAND DOLLAR	★		★	★	★★	★★	★★
98	SAND HOPPER	★★	★	★			
	SCALLOPS						
74	Rock		★	★	★	★	★
73	*Pecten* (swimming)		★	★	★	★	★
	SEA ANEMONES						
120	Brooding			★	★★	★★	★★	★★
20	Green		★★	★	★		
18, 21, 49	Rough green		★★★	★★★	★★★	★★★	★★★	★
138	Sun			★	★	★★	★★	★★
68, 139	*Tealia*		★	★	★	★	★
	SEA CUCUMBERS						
61	Chitonlike		★	★	★	★	★
93	California				★★	★★	★
58, 59	Orange		★★	★★	★★	★★	★★	★
60	White		★★	★★	★★	★★	★★	★

Figure	Species	Outer Coast Sandy	Outer Coast Rocky	Strait of Juan de Fuca	San Juan Islands	Hood Canal	Puget Sound North/South
	SEA LOUSE (Isopod)						
14	Gray	**					
56	Green	**	**	**	**	**	**
117	SEA PEN					*	*	*
	SEA URCHINS						
76	Green				**	**	**	**
41	Purple	**	*	*			
7	Red		*	*			
	SEAWEED						
13, 21	Brown rockweed	***	***	***	***	***	**
5, 67	Coralline	**	**	*			
119	Eelgrass		*	**	***	***	**
102	Enteromorpha				*	**	**
46	Laminaria	**	*	*	*	*	*
46	Sargassum		*	*	***	**	*
46, 49	Sea lettuce		*	**	***	***	***
	SHRIMP						
92	Broken-back	*	*	*	*	*	*
91	Coon-stripe				*	*	*
109	Ghost				*	*	*
85	Marine crayfish (mud shrimp)				*	*	*
125	Skeleton	*	*	*	*	*	*
	SNAILS						
115	Batillaria				**		
31	Keyhole limpet	*	*	*			
19, 47	Limpets	***	***	***	**	**	*
47	Littorine	***	***	***	**	**	*
83, 84	Moon			*	**	**	*
133	Oyster drill						*
135	Slipper						*
28	Turban	***	**	*			
28, 48	Whelk	**	**	**	**	**	**
	SPONGES						
40, 146	Bread crumb			**	**	**	**
57	Encrusting	**	**	**	**	**	**
33	Red	**	*	*			
	STARFISH						
25	Blood	*	*	*	*	*	
27, 62	Brittle (serpent)	**	**	*	*	*	*
26	Broad disc	*	*	*	*	*	
51	Leather	*	*	*	*	*	
50	Mottled			*	**	**	*
23	Purple (ochre)	***	**	*			
112	Rose			*	*	*	*
24	Six-rayed	**	*	*			
113	Sun				*	*	
111	Sunflower				**	**	

Figure	Species	Outer Coast Sandy	Outer Coast Rocky	Strait of Juan de Fuca	San Juan Islands	Hood Canal	Puget Sound North/South
	TUNICATES						
39, 131	Colonial	★★★	★★	★★	★	★	★
132	Hairy sea squirt	★	★	★	★	★	★
	WORMS						
52	Calcareous	★★	★★	★★	★★	★★	★
110	Glycerid			★	★	★	★
147	Feather-duster			★	★	★	★
55	Flatworms			★	★	★	★
88	Peanut	★	★	★			
87	Pile			★★	★★	★★	★★
54	Ribbon	★	★	★★	★★	★★	★★
31, 86	Scale			★	★★	★★	★
53	Shellbinder			★	★	★	★
148	Shipworm *(Teredo)*	(any submerged wood anywhere)					

154

Table 2

Vertical Distribution of Individual Species Listed in this Book

Key: ••• = abundant •• = common • = occasional blank = absent or rare

Figure	Species	High Tide Zone	Mid-tide Zone	Low Tide Zone	Minus Tides	Subtidal	Floats
29, 30	ABALONE				•	•	
	BARNACLES						
47	Acorn	••	•••				
16	Goose	••					
17, 49	Ribbed		••				
	CHITONS						
24	Leather			•	•		
35	Lined			•	•		
36, 37	Moccasin			•	•		
34	Mossy			•	•		
	CLAMS, Similar Bivalves						
81	Bent-nose			•			
81, 82	Butter			•	••	••	
127	Eastern soft-shell		••				
106, 107	Gweduc				•	•	
118	Heart cockle			•	•	•	
108	Horse			•	•	•	
82	Macoma			•			
82	Manila littleneck		••				
81	Native littleneck			•	•	•	
75	Piddock			•	•	•	
97	Razor			•	••	•	
	CRABS						
65	Black-clawed shore				•	•	
66	Decorator			•	•	•	
103	Dungeness			•	•	••	
137	Graceful cancer			•	•	•	
136	Green shore			••	•		
64	Hairy cancer			•	•		
67	Kelp			•	•		
42	Porcelain			•	•		
63	Purple shore		••	•			
104, 105	Red (rock)			•	•	••	
	FISH						
43, 44	Clingfish			•	•		
77	Cockscomb prickleback			•	•	•	
123	Penpoint gunnel (blenny)			•	•	•	
94, 95	Tide pool sculpin	•	••				
22, 89, 90, 124	HERMIT CRABS	•	•	•	•		

Figure	Species	High Tide Zone	Mid-tide Zone	Low Tide Zone	Minus Tides	Subtidal	Floats
140, 141	HYDROIDS			●	●	●	●●●
	JELLYFISH						
139	Sea blubber			(open water)			●
144	Sea gooseberry (comb jelly)			(open water)			●
121	Stalked			●			
143	Thimble			(open water)			●
142	Water			(open water)			●
	KELP						
15	Sea palm	●●					
46	Seal head (bladder)			●	●	●●	
	MUSSELS						
49	Bay		●●	●●			
17	California		●●	●			
	NUDIBRANCHS						
70	*Cadlina*			●	●		
72	*Dendronotus*			●	●	●	
114	Frosted			●	●	●	
145	Opalescent			●	●	●	●●
122	*Phyllaplysia* (sea slug)			●	●		
33	Red			●	●		
69	Sea lemon			●	●	●	
32	Spotted (ringed)			●	●		
71	*Triopha*			●	●	●	
78	OCTOPUS			●	●	●	
	OYSTERS						
131	Native (Olympia)			●			
130	Pacific (Japanese)			●			
58	Rock (jingle shell)			●			
116	SAND DOLLAR			●	●	●	
98	SAND HOPPER	●●	●	●	●	●	●
	SCALLOPS						
74	Rock				●	●	
73	*Pecten* (swimming)				●	●	
	SEA ANEMONES						
120	Brooding			●	●		
20	Green			●	●		
18, 21, 49	Rough green		●●	●			
138	Sun			●	●	●●	●●●
68, 139	*Tealia*			●	●	●	
	SEA CUCUMBERS						
61	Chitonlike			●	●		
93	California			●	●	●	
58, 59	Orange			●	●	●	
60	White			●	●	●	

156

Figure	Species	High Tide Zone	Mid-tide Zone	Low Tide Zone	Minus Tides	Subtidal	Floats
	SEA LOUSE (Isopod)						
14	Gray	●					
56	Green		●	●			●
117	SEA PEN			●	●	●●	
	SEA URCHINS						
76	Green			●	●	●	
41	Purple			●	●		
7	Red			●	●		
	SEAWEED						
13, 21	Brown rockweed		●●				
5, 67	Coralline		●	●	●	●	
119	Eelgrass		●	●●	●		
102	*Enteromorpha*		●●				
46	*Laminaria*			●●	●●	●●	
46	*Sargassum*			●	●●	●●	
46, 49	Sea lettuce		●	●●●	●		
	SHRIMP						
92	Broken-back			●	●		
91	Coon-stripe			●	●	●●	
109	Ghost			●	●		
85	Marine crayfish (mud shrimp)			●	●		
125	Skeleton			●	●		●●
	SNAILS						
115	*Batillaria*		●	●			
31	Keyhole limpet			●	●		
19, 47	Limpets		●●	●●			●
47	Littorine	●●	●				
83, 84	Moon			●	●	●	
133	Oyster drill			●	●		
135	Slipper			●	●		
28	Turban		●●				
28, 48	Whelk		●	●●			
	SPONGES						
40, 146	Bread crumb			●●	●		●●
57	Encrusting			●	●		
33	Red			●	●		
	STARFISH						
25	Blood			●	●	●	
27, 62	Brittle (serpent)			●	●	●	
26	Broad disc			●	●	●	
51	Leather			●	●	●	
50	Mottled			●●	●		
23	Purple (ochre)		●●	●			
112	Rose			●	●	●	
24	Six-rayed			●	●		
113	Sun			●	●	●	
111	Sunflower			●	●	●	

Figure	Species	High Tide Zone	Mid-tide Zone	Low Tide Zone	Minus Tides	Subtidal	Floats
	TUNICATES						
39, 131	Colonial			●	●		●●
132	Hairy sea squirt			●	●	●	●
	WORMS						
52	Calcareous			●●	●●	●	●●
110	Glycerid			●	●		
147	Feather-duster			●	●	●	●●
55	Flatworms		●●	●			
88	Peanut			●	●		
87	Pile		●	●			
54	Ribbon			●	●	●	
31, 86	Scale			●	●	●	
53	Shellbinder			●	●		
148	Shipworm (*Teredo*)		(any submerged wood)				●●

KEY TO TERMS

High Tide Zone — approximately the upper third of the beach, which is exposed on an average low tide.

Mid-tide Zone — the third of the beach approximately halfway between extreme high tide and extreme low tide. Brown rockweed is a good indicator of this level on a rocky beach.

Low Tide Zone — approximately the lower third of the beach. This region always includes the zero tide level, which is defined in the United States as the average of the lowest tide each day over as many years as there are data. In Canada, zero tide level is the average of the lowest tide of each month for which there are records. It is about two feet lower than the United States zero.

Minus Tide Region — that portion of the low tide zone at a height less than the zero defined above. This region is given special emphasis in this book to point out that there are some subtidal animals which can be seen intertidally only during very low (minus) tides.

Subtidal — below the lowest tide.

Float — a specific habitat on a floating object, which is never uncovered and is usually in protected waters.

158

Other Pacific Search Books in Paperback

The Carrot Cookbook by Ann Saling. Over 200 mouth-watering recipes. 160 pp. $3.50.

The Dogfish Cookbook by Russ Mohney. Over 65 piscine delights. Cartoons and drawings. 108 pp. $1.95.

Fire and Ice: The Cascade Volcanoes by Stephen L. Harris. Copublished with The Mountaineers. 275 pp. $7.50.

The Green Tomato Cookbook by Paula Simmons. More than 80 solutions to the bumper crop. 96 pp. $2.95.

Minnie Rose Lovgreen's Recipe for Raising Chickens by Minnie Rose Lovgreen. 2nd edition. 32 pp. $2.00.

Sleek & Savage: North America's Weasel Family by Delphine Haley. Extraordinary color and black-and-white photos; bibliography. 128 pp. $5.50.

Toothed Whales: In Eastern North Pacific and Arctic Waters compiled by Alice Seed. 2nd edition. 40 pp. $1.75.

Why Wild Edibles? The Joys of Finding, Fixing, and Tasting – West of the Rockies by Russ Mohney. Color and black-and-white photos plus illustrations. 320 pp. $6.95.

Wild Mushroom Recipes by the Puget Sound Mycological Society. 2nd edition. Over 200 recipes. 178 pp. $6.95.

The Zucchini Cookbook by Paula Simmons. Revised and enlarged 2nd edition. Over 150 tasty creations. 160 pp. $3.50.

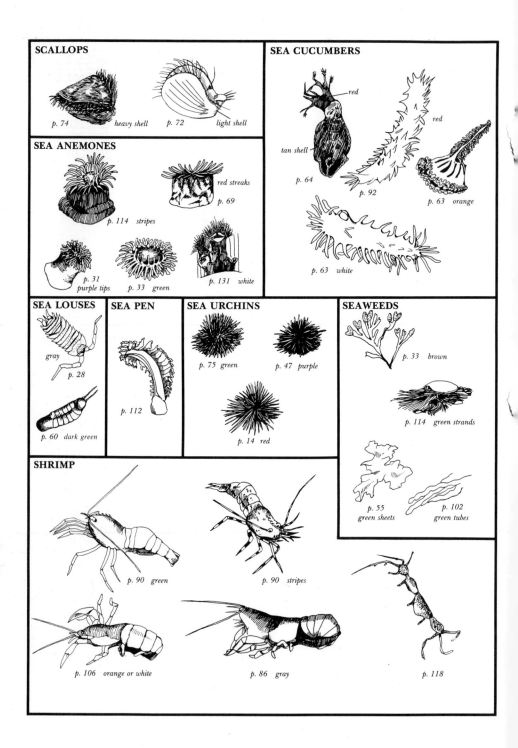

SCALLOPS

p. 74 heavy shell p. 72 light shell

SEA CUCUMBERS

red

tan shell

red

p. 64 p. 92 p. 63 orange

p. 63 white

SEA ANEMONES

red streaks

p. 69

p. 114 stripes

p. 31 purple tips p. 33 green p. 131 white

SEA LOUSES

gray

p. 28

p. 60 dark green

SEA PEN

p. 112

SEA URCHINS

p. 75 green p. 47 purple

p. 14 red

SEAWEEDS

p. 33 brown

p. 114 green strands

p. 55 green sheets p. 102 green tubes

SHRIMP

p. 90 green p. 90 stripes

p. 106 orange or white p. 86 gray p. 118